WHAT DOESN'T KILL YOU MAKES YOU STRONGER

April Ramos

"Tough times don't last; tough people do."
- Robert H. Schuller

Dedication

I would like to dedicate this book to my son Maddox. You have taught me the true definition of love and to be loved unconditionally. You have taught me so much and have become my reason to exist. You are my heart living outside of my body. I know my story is not going to be an easy read, but honey, life is not intended to be easy. It is what we do about the hard moments that gets us through. It is how you respond that truly matters to the harshness of life. We get knocked down, we fight, we get back up and do it all over again. It is the never giving up that matters. That is what makes a story others would want to read.

Contents

Acknowledgments

A profound thank you to all the doctors and nurses who helped save my life. Most especially my Doctor Sean Mullally and nurse Robin Clark. I truly believe I would not be here today if it was not for the two of you providing loving care and swift actions that surely saved my life. You both cared for me with such grace and dedication. Any patient who comes into your care is absolutely fortunate beyond measure.

I would like to thank my mother, who stopped her life completely to take care of me and nursed me back to life with her nourishment, humor, and sass. I am indebted to her for jumping down the rabbit hole of suffering with me and still coming out just as gracefully on the other side with me. We have had many long nights of pain, misery, and the unknowing gnawing at us with all the uncertainties that lay ahead of us, suffocating our thoughts and crippling our voices. God knew what he was doing pairing the two of us up. You will never know how strong you have to be until you do not have a choice.

I am deeply grateful to the family and friends who have nurtured and loved me during my hardest times in life and found the strength to lift me up when I needed it the most. There are too many to list; I can only say you know who you are. I would like to acknowledge a special thank you to my Aunt Kimberly Strange, who worked very hard to give me a successful benefit that saved me from losing everything I worked so hard for.

I would like to express my sincere gratitude to my two step-fathers who helped raise me tough. You both have pushed me harder than anyone else in my life to make something of myself. You taught me tough love can get the job done. Thank you both for always showing up for me and loving me unconditionally like your own.

Thank you to my dog Lady, who sat on my feet during long writing nights. You can blame her for any typos. It was because of you that I worked twice as hard to make it back.

A special thank you to my miracle son Maddox, who is now twelve years old. You keep my heart tender and full of love for all the remaining years of my life. You are the bright light that came from the darkest of nights. You are beautiful, kind, sweet, and so full of love that your bucket spills over to anyone who is blessed to know you.

Baby, you broke the mold!

Introduction

"I'm writing this so you can read my thoughts in the event my lips can't find the energy to speak." These are the first words I wrote in my notebooks that I'd leave for my mother to read when I passed away. It was almost impossible to survive my cancer, and I knew this. I felt it. I wanted to tell her so much, but I just didn't have the energy. It hurt to communicate. It made me weaker. I needed to build up my strength. I needed to store the energy and use it when I really had to, like going to the bathroom. Or shoveling food in my mouth.

These words grew from one page to several pages until they became multiple notebooks. I wrote most of this book in tiny cliff notes placed messily in a pocket-sized journal that could easily fit in the back of my jeans or a clutch purse while I was either on the go or home stuck with my thoughts. These tiny journals filled with chicken scratch made me feel heard and validated, even when I didn't have the strength to talk. I did not realize it until later, much later, when all my notes began to add up together, that I would be writing a book.

Even while the mind feels like it is slowly failing you, it can think of the most magical things. Words have the power to free you from the chains of silence. Like Buddha teaches, suffering is an inevitable part of life, necessary in order to know what happiness means. Happiness is not defined by the absence of pain, but by how we respond to the unavoidable hardships of existence.

This memoir is my legacy after I perish. Because we all know that day will one day come. Unfortunately, death will want to come for me sooner than I anticipate. Beginnings are scary, endings are usually sad, but it's what's in the middle that counts.

Chapter 1 – Live Like You Are Dying

Most days are unremarkable; they begin and end within a twenty-four-hour expanse and have no lasting memories in between. Most days have no impact on the course of a life. March 22nd was a Monday, and the events that happened that day would change my life forever. It started off as any regular day would, any regular day for a sick person that is.

I had a hard time sleeping the night before as I had for the fourteen nights prior. I was averaging a total of about three hours of sleep a night.

I had just gotten back from San Diego two days before my mother's birthday, leaving me with a day in between to attend the big Holyoke parade which I attended every year seven miles north of Springfield. From ages nineteen to twenty-one when I didn't live in Springfield, I lived within walking distance from the route of the parade in Holyoke itself. Massachusetts stages the United States' second largest annual St. Patrick's Day Parade, only slightly smaller than New York's. The parade averaged approximately 400,000 viewers the past few years.

When my friend Harry and I originally booked our tickets to San Diego we planned on coming back in time so we wouldn't miss this event. I remember feeling drained and not well enough to be surrounded by this many people. I felt uncomfortable and contained the anxiety running rampant inside of me. I kept telling myself I was just jet-lagged from the 2,500-mile plane trip. I felt like I needed longer and better sleep, but I knew as soon as my head hit that pillow it would be an impossible task. It was almost like my body forgot how to fall asleep. I felt tired and restless but falling asleep wasn't easy, especially with all the coughing. And on top of it I was severely constipated, different from your garden variety constipation that I had felt from time to time. In San Diego I even missed our first jet ski appointment because I couldn't get off the toilet. I was sweating profusely and thought I may pass out. I finally passed a small stool. They always say it is very important to go number two for your body. If not you are poisoning yourself leaving these toxins in. I never did a good job with waste management internally, but I knew now something must be terribly wrong.

So what did I do? I stuck it out. I stayed for the whole parade. I did not drink, so I offered to be the designated driver. All I had was one Jell-O shot so I could feel something smooth and cold go down my raw throat. Everyone was asking me how California was, yet I didn't have the breath or energy to replay back my vacation to my friends. I was short and spoke in almost incomplete sentences trying to bring up key, fun, and important experiences. I told the same stories to everyone. I said I met up with some friends, Chris who was stationed as a Navy officer, and his girlfriend at the time Krystal. I told them I went kayaking in the sea, and jet skiing. I saw a No Doubt cover band called No Duh and attended a St. Patrick's Day Festival. Everything else I left up to their imaginations.

When you're really sick, you find a way of making excuses for your symptoms so you feel justified not going to the ER then waiting a half a day for them to tell you once again that, "you have bronchitis." In the past three months I went to a few local hospitals in Springfield on three separate occasions looking for the answers as to why my body ached, why my cough hadn't subsided, and why I couldn't catch my breath, along with all the other symptoms my body was experiencing. This had been on-going since the middle of last year, approximately six months prior to my fateful day.

March 22nd, 2010 was supposed to be a wonderful planned out day. It was my mother's forty-ninth birthday and we were ready to celebrate it the best way we knew how, with lobsters and movies.

I'm her only child; it's always just been us. I arrived at my mother's house a little groggy but trying my hardest to be chipper and happy for her birthday. I welcomed her with all the souvenirs I collected that reminded me of her.

Ever since I was a kid people have always told me how beautiful my mother is. As a child I loved my mother unconditionally, and I still do. I always thought she was a goddess. She was my everything. She has long, straight dirty blonde hair with natural sun highlights that glisten every time she moves her head. She has soft green, empathetic eyes, which she decorates with black eyeliner and mascara. She stands at five-foot-one and weighs approximately one hundred and thirty pounds. And her body curves in all the right places.

She had me at twenty-three so she's not as old as some of the other moms I know, but she's been around long enough to see something go in with fashion to only come back around again. Her body resembled Heather Locklear. But her hair was more like Tommy Lee's.

As a kid we would go on so many long weekend adventures trying to escape the immediate area and search for the ocean, any bit of water we could find. I was spoiled being the only child but I guess that's a common thing to say. I've always felt like it's my mother and I against the world, and I love that.

The minute I walked into the house on her birthday she took one look at me and knew something was wrong. I remember seeing her approach me at the door with strong squared off shoulders and a Ronald McDonald smile. But in a matter of seconds her posture disintegrated into worry and concern.

I remember thinking, *uh oh what did I do?*

"What's wrong with your face?" she asked.

I felt relieved yet hurt at the same time. She immediately took my pulse thinking that it was my ticker acting up again. After a minute she seemed pleased to know my heart wasn't showing any signs of distress.

"How are you feeling?" she asked while embracing me in a hug.

With my mom I always tell her the truth. "I feel like shit and this bronchitis is kicking my ass."

I settled in a little; she opened her gifts and we started a movie before we planned on heading out and picking up some lobsters at her local Wal-Mart.

While watching the movie she noticed how hard it was for me to catch my breath between spurts of coughing. "You need to call your doctor's office and ask them what they think."

Like a good daughter, I obeyed. After describing my symptoms and practically hacking up a lung on the phone, my doctor felt it was unusual for me to have a persisting cough and suggested that I go to the emergency room to get a chest X-ray just to make sure I hadn't come down with pneumonia.

I got off the phone and gave my mom a look like, *Really? You want me to go to the ER right now!?* She gave me a smirk and I knew it was her day so whatever she wanted she'd have and whatever she said would go. If it was any other day I wouldn't have gone. I hate hospitals.

I always referred to myself as that old guy that never went for checkups. Then before he knew it, after his first doctor's appointment in years they'd find a bunch of things wrong with him then throw out a short life expectancy sentence for his negligence. I always thought I would rather not know than have paperwork to fill out every time I'd check in somewhere, which I already had to do anyhow from all my prior health complications.

I asked her if she felt like going to the hospital on her birthday but she insisted that my health was more important. We paused the movie and went to her small local hospital hoping to make it in and out and still have time to pick up lobsters on the way back. Man, were we wrong.

My mother is a local EMT in town so she said hello to a bunch of doctors and nurses as we walked in and made small talk. As soon as I got in, I was already bored with the idea of being there. I'm sure my body language showed it, but I pepped up after remembering it was my mother's birthday and I should probably make the best of it. I started joking around with the staff trying to make light of the situation and amuse my mom as much as I could.

I described all my symptoms and got into a gurney and took some chest X-rays. As we were waiting for what seemed like forever in our own personal 10x10 waiting room, I started goofing off a little. I tend to appreciate the little things like sticky glue that comes on the back of a mailed debit card. I usually get more excited about that than the card itself. It can keep me entertained for hours. I still had some stuff mailed to my mother's house and found a few credit card offers in the mail which I brought to the hospital to open up. I started joking around pretending the sticky glue resembled boogers while sticking them up one of my nostrils. I was trying to kill time and make light of the situation (did I already mention I hate hospitals?). I remember asking my mom to take a picture quickly because it wouldn't stick long. I even asked her how many calories she thought boogers had. She said five to ten, depending on the pickings.

Our laughs soon turned into muffled giggles as the ER doctor walked into the room with a serious look on his face. My heart most definitely skipped a beat. Here I was filling this closet-sized room full of laughter and this guy comes strolling in with the look of death on his face on my mom's birthday. I mean who was this guy? He couldn't crack a smile? I know he saw the fake booger and my sense of humor is intoxicating (or so I hear).

Then he dropped the bomb and said he now needed an emergency CAT scan.

"What is going on?" my mom asked with concern.

"I need to get a clearer look," the stone-cold doctor said.

"Does it look like pneumonia?" Mom asked.

"It looks a little bit like something but I can't be quite sure yet."

"A like a little bit like what?" she asked growing frustrated with the man.

"It could be like lymphoma but we're still not sure yet."

I being illiterate in this conversation thought lymphoma, pneumonia, they kinda rhyme. Maybe lymphoma is just pneumonia's kissing cousin. How bad could this be? With no time to waste, like a little puppy in trouble, I followed him down the hall with my tail in between my legs. I looked back once more at my mom's face as I passed the door frame; she lost all color in her face. I knew right then and there I was screwed.

After more scanning and lots more time I eventually made it back to the waiting room and found my mother and now stepfather waiting for me. *Why did she call him?* I thought. Then I saw my first pity face. I didn't know how to describe it at first. I thought, *why is he so sad?* Then I realized he had been crying and now he was trying to hold back his tears as he gave me a great big hug. I realized that maybe this wasn't a look of pity. This man was scared. This was the first time I saw a man scared in my entire life.

This was also one of the first times that I had seen a grown man cry, and the first time a grown man was crying for me. I felt touched and worried at the same time. How do you comfort someone when you need to be comforted? Now I was worried. I saw my mom trying to be the strong advocate in the room. I realized they immediately changed roles. She must have told him bad news but I hadn't even heard the bad news yet. I was confused and then upset that nobody was telling me what was going on with me!

I sat there and became perfectly still as a statue and felt cold and stiff like one as well. I watched my mother leave and reenter the room a few times trying to collect herself. My brain was off somewhere else. I went into another state of consciousness. I was there physically, yes, but mentally I was nowhere and everywhere at the same time. My mind would race and then come to a sudden stop and stay there for a bit. It was as if I were being trapped into different plains within my mind. Whenever someone asked me a question it brought me back up to speed with what I was missing around me. Then my brain went into fast forward mode. I was not able to catch up. I missed everything that was happening around me in those minutes.

My body was in such bad shape, I can only describe it as indigo. Indigo is the sixth color of the rainbow that just barely exists. I barely existed at that point.

This wasn't the first time my brain had gone to this place. I think it's a safety mechanism that I was programmed with. Outside the waiting room through my agony bubble I saw all the nurses and the doctors talking amongst each other out of earshot. They would look back in my direction with a shocked, sad face and then proceeded to go on their merry way with whatever mission they had next.

Right then and there I knew I was in bad shape before I even had a chance to hear it for myself. I felt like everyone in the hospital knew before I did. I couldn't tell you how long it took for the doctor to return with a specialist to tell us exactly what was going on with me. They finally dumbed it down for me and explained to me that they found lumps in my chest.

He starts to discuss the lumps. I immediately cut him off while letting out a slight, nervous chuckle. I was trying to stay optimistic, explaining to them that that's a relief and nothing to be alarmed for because I, in fact, have fibrocystic breast disease.

I've had lumps in my chest for a while now. Fibrocystic breast disease is usually benign and affects about thirty to sixty percent of woman. It is primarily found in women thirty years of age or older. Mammograms usually discover this for most. I found my large lumps when I was in middle school. These types of lumps will move if you push on them. They do not feel stuck or fixed to anything.

My symptoms and pain with them is worse right before a menstrual cycle. They feel heavy, swollen, and very sensitive to the touch. This happens in the glandular breast tissue, where the production, or the secretion, of milk of the breast duct becomes blocked; possibly from your body producing too much estrogen without the opportunity to break it down in a reasonable amount of time before your body produces more by your next menstrual cycle.

They both looked at each other, then back at me again. The specialist chimed in. "No, the lumps are surrounding your lungs and heart."

In the human body, your left lung is smaller than your right lung to make room in your chest cavity for your heart. Inside me there was a large mass starting from the bottom of my right lung spiraling into the top of my heart. It was playing a tug of rope game in the middle of my chest with my organs.

I think that when you hear really bad news you go through the same type of stages you do when a close loved one dies.

Immediately I went into denial. They then told me that their hospital wasn't equipped with the care that I would need. They called in an ambulance to rush me to Baystate Hospital which was better equipped to handle my type of cancer and to give me a proper diagnosis. That's when I finally heard it! I even asked myself; *did he just say cancer?*

Oh my God this can't be! I then attempted to call their bluff. I told them I wasn't going to go anywhere unless they showed me this "so called tumor."

At first they seemed hesitant. Maybe they were in shock from my aggressive response. After a few seconds they both gave a sad nod.

The first doctor arranged for a nurse down the hall to greet me and relayed my demands. Together we went to the nurses' ER office and began pulling up my CAT scan on the screen. This was the nurse that initially greeted us when we came in and got us situated. She had a small frame. I remember thinking she had a pretty face, and I liked her dirty blonde curly hair that looked wild as can be. I glanced down; sure enough she had a wedding ring. *Lucky guy*, I thought. There it was again, the pity face, the face I never knew before and the one I would soon love to hate.

I kept my head high staying in this denial stage as long as I could. They had to be wrong. They must be wrong. Maybe it's someone else's X-rays that they got mixed up with mine. I figured I'd look for clues on the X-ray that would show it wasn't me. It couldn't be me. Then the nurse who was happy and vibrant before seemed dull and mousy. I hated her for that. I didn't like the feeling of people feeling bad for me. It's a role I never had to play before.

As soon as the image came up on the computer screen my heart finally sank. I went into a minor shock; a deer in headlights kind of shock. There was the reality of the situation bright as day staring back at me. I suddenly didn't know what to do. I was looking at what was supposed to resemble a chest that distinguishes your multiple different organs, but all I saw was one large solid mass connecting all the dots together. It looked terrible and it looked like it got the best of my lungs. My stomach threw itself in knots. If we did indeed eat lobster before this, I most likely would have lost it at this point and wasted my favorite dish.

Chapter 2 - Waaambulance

The ambulance arrived before I was even able to say anything. The nurse who pulled up the screen hugged me and said something in my ear that made me irate. "I'd really like to know how this turns out for you." Really? I thought this woman would be searching for me in the obituaries for the next few days. I thought it was a heartless thing to say. But who knows what the right thing to say is during a time like that?

The petite female EMT then shuffled me into the ambulance as I heard muffled broken words from my mother saying that she would be following the ambulance with her car and would be right behind me the whole way.

The minute those ambulance doors shut behind me I lost it. I totally freaked out in the presence of a stranger. For the record, this was the first of two times that I had ever freaked out about my disease, each time lasted for about a total of fifteen minutes.

I started to enter my anger stage at this point, a stage I wouldn't leave for about three weeks. I started yelling, "why me?" Followed by "What did I ever do to deserve this?" which I screamed to no one in particular. I then began stating facts to the poor EMT about how I was the kind of person who has dedicated her life to helping others and that I didn't deserve this. After the yelling subsided a bit the EMT started poking around into my head trying to find hints as to what my first symptoms were. Maybe she felt she could discover the secret combination of symptoms that brought me there that day.

I know all the doctors and nurses felt badly because I was so young for my life to come to a screeching halt the way that it had. For me to find out this late in the game that I had cancer, the Grim Reaper was already knocking at my door. They felt so strongly about this that they decided the first person that should greet me at my next hospital spot should be a priest so I could say my goodbyes.

After I was done throwing a temper tantrum I calmed down and apologized. "I can't let my mother see me this upset when we get to the hospital," I said through tears. I looked out the back of the ambulance window and sure enough Mom was there, just as she promised about two car lengths behind us keeping up speed. I tried to see if I could make out her facial expressions. I wanted to know if she was keeping it together better than I was, or was she utilizing this time to fall apart knowing I wasn't in her company?

Bob, my step-dad, drove his own truck to meet us at the hospital. I remember thinking of him and feeling guilty because I knew he had to get up early for work the next morning and it was already 10:00 p.m. at this point. My brain was going all over the place fueled by anger from my half-assed diagnosis. I was also *hangry* on top of it. The nightmare hadn't even started yet and I already wanted it to stop. I thought to myself, *where did that original doctor get his degree, eBay?* The human brain thinks about seventy thousand thoughts on an average day. I knew I was putting my brain in overload this particular day.

For the first time in my life I wanted to be someone else. I didn't want to be in this body. I didn't want to have these thoughts. I didn't want to be where I was. I didn't want these moments to exist. And I certainly didn't want this young EMT to keep drilling me with questions. She wasn't making matters easier for me. Didn't she get it? I wanted a fifteen minute pity party and she wasn't playing along.

This was the only time I self-loathed about my disease and just wanted to fall apart, especially in the presence of a stranger, and she was ruining it! I remember wishing she would climb up into the front of the ambulance and let me break down in peace. I had a bunch of friends that worked for the same ambulance company. I remember hoping this girl didn't remember my name because I didn't want her to relay my depressing story to others including the people I knew who she worked with.

That ambulance ride felt so long and tedious I didn't know what to do with myself. The world felt heavy and was coming down on me and I just wanted to run and hide. Maybe being trapped in this vehicle was making things all too real. It was bringing me to the present even though my mind wanted desperately to escape.

Finally we arrived at our destination, good old Baystate Medical Center. As soon as the EMTs were taking the stretcher out of the ambulance I saw my mom. She didn't skip a beat and was right there by my side. In fact, the only time she left me during this whole ordeal was when she had followed the ambulance in her own vehicle. Till this day she still goes to every doctor's appointment with me.

I honestly believe this woman was meant to be my mother. I always wondered if all mothers were like her or if I was born to a super mother. Maybe it's just a mother's natural instinct to narrow in on what's important. Or maybe it was all those years of medical work paying off. She has been an EMT for almost twenty years and has worked many other jobs in the medical field as well.

She has saved many people just by finding out her patient's symptoms by working down from the most extreme thing that could be wrong with them to the most common. EMTs are the first responders and the decisions they make can cost a patient their life. Her methods show how compassionate of a woman she truly is with a drive to save others.

As they were wheeling me into the hospital, I was immediately confronted by a priest waiting for me at the entrance door. I was confused. Who is this tall, gray-haired old man standing before me, now proceeding to walk beside me as we're rolling closer to my doom. He started talking but I was easily distracted by my thoughts still trying to escape the immediate situation. Not to mention I was a little cold and still strapped in. *I don't like this one bit*, I thought to myself. He was so soft-spoken. I couldn't catch anything he was saying. His words were definitely not louder than my own thoughts screaming in my head.

Would it have been such a horrible decision to have them stop around the next corner so I could get out and walk away? Couldn't I refuse treatment at this time? My mom came with her car so we could still technically leave, right? My brain was cluttered with ways to escape as his words are all coming to a halt outside my eardrums because I was refusing to let them in. Who was this guy and why was he talking to me? Was it so late in the day that he had no other patient to talk to? Or was he the priest on door duty greeting every patient who gets stretchered in by ambulance?

Finally my voice broke through my thoughts. *Who are you?* He proceeded to explain himself and then asked me what religion I followed. I tried to tell him through bits of coughs that I believed in all religions and I was more of a spiritual person. I didn't belong to any one religion in particular but I was baptized Catholic.

"I want to make you feel comfortable with my religion," he said and then told me he was the only religious person working at this hour. "It might take a while to get someone else in here to see you."

I really wanted a Buddhist representative but I figured he'd do until then. They special ordered me a Buddhist priest via paperwork, or so I was told at the time. I thought that was pretty cool. Then the reality set in and hit me like a ton of communion wafers. Wait a minute...they ordered me a priest to say my good-byes? What?! This was right out of a scene from a sappy movie.

The tears started streaming down my face and I started to choke up quite a bit. Is this what's really happening to me right now? Is this where the end of my life took me? This can't be! Somebody made a mistake somewhere. They got the wrong girl! Here comes the denial stage again but this time I kept it to myself. I looked over to my mom and stepdad who just entered the room. They looked just as lost and empty as I felt.

After hearing the word "cancer" yet again by the fourth doctor I realized I was most likely going to be here a while and wouldn't be going home any time soon. The reality hit that I had bills to pay and places to be tomorrow. I was supposed to be at all of my jobs for the next few weeks with no days off in between. I had just used all of my vacation time, allowing myself to get settled back in before my busy week started up again.

What was I going to tell work? My clients relied on me. I was needed outside of this hospital room. I left that job to my mother, who was eager to make the call outside for me with my cell phone while she got to suck down another cigarette. I wondered what she was going to say to them. Was she going to use the word "cancer?"

The priest stayed with me until the wee hours of the morning. "I really hope there is a heaven up there," I said to the priest. "If not, there is a lot of wasted space." It took a while for a team of two doctors to come to see me. I think they wanted to make a plan as to what they wanted to do with me. The nurses kept showing up regularly to check my vitals while asking questions.

I don't remember much else from this time. I felt so drained from all the emotions running through me. I think I started to block out the memories as a self-defense mechanism or maybe I went into a minor shock from all the negative information overload. Either way, I lost a part of me in that emergency room that I will never get back.

Sickness is a great equalizer and doesn't attack just the poor or the rich; it treats everyone the same.

I went into that emergency room as April Ramos and came out an entirely different person, a cancer patient. I woke up from a bad dream and into a bad dream. I was groggy; my brain thirsty for sleep.

I have never been a coffee person. I have a heart condition labeled as first degree heart block where my electrical impulses misfire. So as part of this condition I have to stay away from everything that could speed up my heart, things like caffeine, chocolate, and any uppers. So I had no way of relieving my fatigue.

The clock turned twelve and unlike Cinderella or her pump-kin carriage, I did not turn into anything other than myself. The doctors settled me into my own room in the ICU and encouraged my mother to go home, get some rest, and come back with some clothes for the days to follow. She was not allowed to use my shower in my room and I knew she was dying for a cigarette.

After much hesitation she couldn't resist anymore. They had appointed me my own nurse who was ordered to watch over me all night. I was given strict instructions to try and rest. I believe they gave me some Benadryl after I explained that I had not slept in two weeks. While lying in my room, I remember thinking it was very small and I was glad to have it all to myself. It was just big enough for one bed and chair. The chair was loud, the only obnoxious thing in the room. I had a television off in the upper corner, and my own small private bathroom. The television was either off, on mute, or I just didn't pay attention to it. I felt more comfortable in that small room alone than the big busy Emergency Room that I had to share with a dozen other people. It was quiet and I was able to think better and somewhat calm down.

One of my newly appointed doctors, a small Indian lady, explained to me that they were going to schedule a biopsy in the morning in my neck region. This way they could get a sample of the type of tumor that grew inside of me so they could better understand how to treat it. She encouraged me to get some much-needed rest.

I finally drifted into sleep land when I got woken up by a bunch of cackling. I was so mad. I really needed that sleep. I looked out into the hallway and it was my nurse partying it up with other nurses at their nest with a pizza box having a grand old time not trying to keep it down for all the patients surrounding them. I looked at the clock and it was three in the morning. Filled with rage, hunger, and frustration I chucked my puke bucket past my bed, through the door jam, and watched it skid across the floor landing about ten feet away from one of the male nurse's legs.

I thought this is neither the time nor place for their little party. For Christ's sake, didn't they know I was on my death bed? My nurse came in and apologized. I realized I already was not myself and how quickly that happened. Not only five hours ago I was given the terrible news. This wasn't me throwing in the towel already. Or was it?

Chapter 3 - Biopsy

My stepfather had to report to work that next morning, so it was just me and my mother until one of my old best friends entered the room, pulling a large suitcase filled with clothes I hardly ever wore. She beamed with pride, excited to do her part and contribute. My mother must have assigned her this job, I thought. Where did she find these clothes? Then I remembered how much weight I had previously lost and how I just came back from a long trip and it was my day to do laundry.

With suitcase in tow, it looked like I was going on vacation, but that was far from the truth. The electrical pull of life separated my old best friend and I somewhat throughout the years, and we started living separate lifestyles. I was always busy being a full-time college student with a full-time job and a part time job. She was raising a son with her boyfriend.

It was like the Nothing in *NeverEnding Story*. There was a pull of life separating you from those you loved but you just couldn't see it. I lived a single lifestyle and she was starting a family. Growing up we used to work with each other and eventually lived with each other for a few years after she had her son. Now, looking back, I wished I was able to work less and spend more time with them.

In that moment they all were just staring at me, hugging me and then each other. I didn't know what to do or say so the room fell silent until I asked a nurse who came in if I could take a shower. "I don't think so, but I'll go get the doctor and find out.

"Why would you think it would be an issue?" I shot back. "Wouldn't they want that area clean before they make the incision?"

She told me it wasn't up to her to decide, and she'd be right back with my doctor who had the answers.

I just wanted to escape the current moment and a shower seemed like the best place to go. I also wanted to be nice and fresh before the surgery.

The Indian doctor who we met less than twelve hours before and who was as cute as a button entered the room. Her presence demanded respect. I'd never seen such respect for someone so tiny before. Or maybe we all just shut up in suspense because we were thirsty for answers. She explained to me that she would have to make three incisions in my breast and neck region to take multiple samples of the tissue in multiple areas.

I began to beg and plead that she leave my breasts alone and try to make one small incision in a non-noticeable location. Before she had a chance to answer me, I then asked her about how big each incision would be. She said it would be between one and two inches.

I threw my shoulders up and shivered at the thought. "Well, there goes my somewhat perfect boobs," I said to myself. These would also be my first stitches.

The doctor then said she would see what she could do about my request for one incision.

This is where my mother chimed in asking questions. "Isn't it bad to open a person up and leak air into their cancerous tumors?" my mom asked. "Won't that cause it to spread further?

Keep in mind this was when we really had no knowledge or education about cancer. The doctor told us that that is simply not true and is a common myth she hears from her cancer patients. Without testing a sample of the tumor there was no way to know how to treat it. She went on to explain that every type of cancer has its own protocol with how it needs to be diminished.

After hearing this we both just nodded our heads in silence and accepted the facts as fast as they were being thrown at us. I started to get nervous. All of this was too much in such a short amount of time. After I got my approval I jumped into the shower.

Not even minutes into my shower I collapsed and completely lost it. I started to cry hard hoping the water would disguise my tears and drown out my howling. This was the second time I lost it and the last. I started to talk to God again. Not asking Him, "why me" this time but instead I asked Him to watch over me and my loved ones and give strength to those who were closest to me. To make sure to keep an eye on my mother and keep her strong no matter what my outcome was. I made no prayers for myself in particular. I was too worried and concerned for others. I figured I was on whatever path the Lord wanted me on, so I'd accept it. After all, the damage was done, right?

I remembered my mother telling me a few different times that if something happened to me then she wouldn't be long behind me, implying that she would leave this world also. This is what scared me most. After I was done with my wish list she walked into the bathroom and opened the shower curtain with all her clothes on except her shirt. She started to hold me through the outside of the shower, getting her bra wet. I immediately built my strength back up and kept my cool. I didn't want to worry her any more than she already was or get her soaked just because I was feeling weak. I told her I was fine and I'd be right out.

I then told God that I would be okay with Him taking me as long as he kept her safe. I went through the motions of cleaning myself, dried myself off, and put my hospital gurney and non-slip complimentary socks back on and proceeded to open the bathroom door to head back to my room. To my amazement all of my aunts and uncles on my mom's side were there. They all were so quiet anticipating my arrival I didn't even know they were there. A wide array of feelings were bubbling under the surface at this point. I was embarrassed thinking they might have heard me lose it. I was shocked that they all fit in my room. I was touched because they all called out of work on a Tuesday. And I was happy to have a support system. Even my most recent ex-boyfriend came to see me.

It's funny the little things you remember during a tragic event. One of my uncles, Stu, one that I was the least close to was there with his new fiancée. She asked me if there's anything I would like. I wasn't sure what, but my response was, "a sham-rock shake from McDonald's." Maybe I thought back subconsciously to the last time I was in the hospital for surgery. When I was sixteen I had my tonsils and adenoids taken out. With this surgery I was smothered with milkshakes, Jell-O, and applesauce. The thought of having another surgery must have sparked some old neurons.

Almost immediately after this my doctor returned with another doctor to retrieve me for my biopsy. I remember thinking, "oh my God I'm not ready for this." Nothing in life had ever truly prepared me for this. She told me I could only bring two people to walk down with me. I didn't know who to pick.

I didn't want to pick one uncle or aunt and not the other. Everyone knew my mom was coming with me. I chose my recent ex-boyfriend (who saved the day for the first time ever). Since he and I had just been hanging out the day before I figured it was a perfect fit.

In no time, I was rolling down the hospital halls in my bed following my doctor to a team of nurses for the hand off. Within this short amount of time my mother and I tried to fill in my ex-boyfriend with everything that happened and everything we knew. I tried my best to be upbeat to make the air thinner. When we arrived, everyone grew quiet except me and the man prepping me for my intubation. I immediately started to ask about my "cocktail" he was preparing. I referred to it as such to lighten the heavy load on my chest and to "make good" with him to hope maybe in return I'd receive special treatment. I felt like the odds were already in my favor considering my cocktail maker knew my mom from her medical career.

He started me up with IVs as I looked deep into his eyes reaching for his soul hoping he would be kind enough to give me enough juice to last me through the surgery "Is it a good cocktail?" I asked with a smile. "What should I expect from it?"

He answered the question but my brain went into overdrive thinking about a million things besides whatever he was saying. My brain started to panic. I realized I hadn't had enough time to mentally prepare for this. I felt my body screaming inside. I grew paralyzed with fear. I opened my mouth to scream, Wait, no! Hang on a second! But nothing came out. My courage was the only thing I had to hang onto for the sake of my mother. I watched in complete shock thinking to myself, *so this is where my life has led me to.*

He then asked me to count backward from ten. My last bit of energy realized that "April Ramos" had left and knew this was her only chance to cry out in fear. I let the words escape my lips as I spoke out loud. "Is it too late to change my mind," I stammered. Then my lights went out.

On Facebook we put our little worlds on blast. In fact, my mother started a prayer group for me that had hundreds of people joining to say a prayer in my name. Before I had cancer my mother didn't even have Facebook. She signed up just to stay connected to everyone posting updates of what was going on with me. She connected with all of my friends. It was easier for her to make a single post rather than answer twenty-five messages. Facebook kept everyone in the loop.

I often had friends sneak booze into the hospital for my mother to help ease her nerves. Whenever anyone asked her if they could bring anything, she always responded, "Yeah Grand Marnier." And they would bring it without blinking an eye knowing that it would help ease the troubles on her heart and mind.

She was a mess. This was by far the worst thing that had ever happened to her. She claimed that was when all her grey hairs came out and she aged ten years. For me it was just a day of sleep. For her a whole century went by.

Chapter 4 - Sleeping Beauty

Next thing I remember is waking up and struggling to gasp for air, thinking I couldn't breathe. *Why can't I breathe?* I thought. *Oh my god, I can't catch air!* I tried to throw my body forward and attempted to open my eyes; then everything went out again.

The next time I woke up was almost a week later. My doctors decided it would be best if they placed me in a medically induced coma as they fed me chemotherapy through a line in my upper thigh to help shrink the tumor. They decided to keep me on a respirator since I was no longer able to breathe on my own.

I woke up with an oxygen mask on my face covering my mouth and nose. It tasted horrible and stale. I struggled to keep my eyes open and they felt like someone was holding them closed. Like weighted shutters refusing to give. Images were coming to me as a blur. I saw everything as a whole image but the more I blinked the more I was able to focus in on these images that were starting to break apart into different entities. As I was coming to, I realized I was surrounded by people moving closer to me, helping me see them better. My arms felt like logs and my body felt paralyzed. I felt confused and groggy. I was uncertain at first of where I was and what I was doing there.

I attempted to take off my oxygen mask to speak. I fumbled for it; I felt like I had noodles for arms. They were Gumby-like in appearance. *Why do I feel so groggy? How long was I out for? Who's here?* Were all the first thoughts going through my brain.

Someone called for the nurse as my mother grew closer. Her face came out clearer the more I blinked. I started to say something as I still had my mask on. My efforts to take it off came to stretching halt as my mother stopped me and advised me to wait for the nurse to make sure it was okay first. My words sounded like I was speaking through a long pipe. It was hard to hear me speak over the oxygen rushing past my ears. So I proceeded to take off the mask again. I thought it was hard for them to hear me since it was hard for me to hear myself. So in between sentences I tried to take off the mask.

I can't remember what I said or if it was significant or not. I do remember trying to talk to a few family members, but they couldn't understand what I was saying. I was unable to speak too loudly because my vocal cords were damaged from the intubation tube. I tried my best to say something recognizable, something recognizable within the English dictionary. But no one seemed to understand me except my mother. She understood everything I was trying to say and repeated it back to me. I had never felt so close to that woman in my life.

After knowing that she understood everything I was saying, tears started to roll down my cheeks as I had my head cocked to the side looking at her. I felt relieved. The worst thing after experiencing a serious surgery is not being able to communicate with your loved ones to find out what happened. You get a sense of urgency, mixed with confusion and panic. I felt so relieved that it brought on tears of joy and excitement for how beautiful this bond between us was. I wonder how she could have possibly understood what I was saying. I then thought of her as being my angel, and the way she looked into my eyes only confirmed it.

As the days went by, I slowly gained my voice back, but for weeks it was distorted. I also woke up to a lot of other surprises as well. Not only was my voice gone but multiple days went by as well.

After the doctors were done performing the biopsy they attempted to take my intubation tube out of my trachea. While this occurred what they feared had come true. I stopped breathing on my own. At this time my tumor grew too big and it finally collapsed my trachea. In an attempt to quickly save my life they tried to shove my oxygen tube back down my windpipe.

I remember this happening. I don't know all the details but I was mentally alert for this experience. I don't know if I was coming to when they tried this, but I do recall struggling to take a breath of air. I remember wondering what was happening and where my mother was.

Little did I know about five hundred feet away my mother was in hysterics. She claims at about the same time I was struggling in my room she felt that there was something wrong far away in hers. She broke down on the hospital floor and started praying and crying.

When I opened my eyes, they were freakishly bloodshot. I had broken most of the blood vesicles in each eye. I instantly started to complain while in a haze that my vagina hurt. The nurse came in to try to explain to me that I had been hooked up to a catheter. Under the delusion of the morphine I started to say that I was a mermaid after taking a look down there. When I told the nurse I was a mermaid my mother sank in her chair and pretended she wasn't there. Once your conscious mind is out of the way, you're free to be a sheer comedic genius.

I then proceeded to think it was a good idea to tell everyone in earshot that I hadn't had sex in two years. I said this over and over again to anyone who would listen. I even told my father who I never talk to. I remember him telling me he didn't want to hear that. I believe everyone else was patient with me and responded with, "uh huh, or yeah?" After all, they must have heard that or that I was a mermaid ten thousand times. That wasn't the end of the wacky things coming out of my mouth. It was just the beginning. Every time I get drunk or come out of a coma (same thing) I talk about my vagina. I make sure everyone can laugh about the jokes of my misfortune.

When they took the catheter out it was almost like I was one of those dolls that talk when you pull the string... and when I say "talk" I really mean "swear." I most likely said every living swear in the book and may have made up a few more.

I have never had morphine before. The moment I was alert enough to understand to tell them to take me off it I did. I would rather the pain. Morphine makes you feel like you are floating around the room, seeing angles at different perspectives. Bits and pieces of hope cluttering the corners. I switched to Tylenol when I could. I have never taken any serious drugs before, and due to my reactions to this drug I immediately would classify it as a serious drug, which should be stopped when possible. There are two types of pain. There is pain that makes you strong and there's useless pain. That's the sort of pain that is only suffering. I had no idea of the ride I had ahead of me. I had no idea how long I would carry this pain with me.

After they put me under to give me a biopsy they ran into complications. They had no choice but try to keep me on a breathing machine and feed my body chemotherapy through a port to try to shrink the tumor crushing my trachea and esophagus. These were all decisions I didn't and couldn't make for myself. My mother had to make these decisions for me. I had assigned her as my power of attorney. They had placed me in a medically induced coma for days with her consent.

When I woke up from my coma I was in excruciating pain from lying in bed for too long. My body felt pain everywhere like I hadn't experienced before. Later I found out it is called Rhabdomyolysis. It's a process that happens when your muscles break down. Lying in one position caused the skeletal muscle cells to break down, which results in the excretion of muscle protein called myoglobin in the urine. The skeletal muscles play a vital role in ensuring movement of the various voluntary muscles in the body. Muscle breakdown is commonly known for giving you dark colored urine, which I was told I had.

At first I thought all the pain was from the chemotherapy since, to me, that was the only thing I knew was different. Then after my muscle spasms started to present themselves, the nurses helped put two and two together to find out where all this pain was coming from. And since I was so athletic before being hospitalized my body took a bigger hit than others who are not as fit.

So they helped try to ease all the pain with morphine. I then started to hallucinate out of my gourd. I was telling my mother that I could see angels floating around the room. I then began hopping between every picture I had in my room. I traveled through them and visited each place depending on the picture's themed background. Come to find out my mother tried to ease my pain by whispering in my ear to go somewhere far away from here (thanks, Mom; it worked).

30

Now with the angels, I asked everyone if they could see them and was disappointed to find out they couldn't. Did it mean I was in between two plains, this world and the next? I'll never know. Have you ever seen the movie *Where Dreams May Come*? What I remember best in those first few days was me drifting alone through the paintings in the room. One was a safari dream and the other was maybe Australia.

I began brushing my fingers along the foreign plants that I had never seen up close with amazement and wonder. Then a lion approached me. He calmly walked right up to me with a long, confident stride and I knew I shouldn't be afraid of him. So I held my hand out as if being greeted by a dog for the first time. It was a remarkable experience. He bowed his head as if we knew each other from another life.

Later, as I was telling a friend who I hadn't seen in years about this moment I realized what it all meant. My best friend George who passed away had always loved lions; in fact, I almost got a lion tattoo as a symbol for him. All of a sudden all the pieces were woven together and I stopped talking and burst into tears. I completely fell apart and in spurts I was able to try to explain why I was so moved after telling the story. I'm sure I had snot dripping out my nose, but no one seemed to mind.

It was a beautiful thing because when I felt so alone and out of my realm I realized I was far from it. He was there comforting me and guiding me through the toughest time of my life. I couldn't believe it.

After doing research I found out that when cancer spreads to other parts of the body and metastasizes it does so because cancer gets into the blood stream to sections where it lodges and then begins to grow.

Cancer is not one disease, but a group of diseases characterized by an abnormal growth of the cells. This abnormality of cell growth can result in lumps, masses, or tumors in the body that are categorized as malignant (meaning cancerous). To distinguish your different cancer type, the name of the cancer refers to the organ or type of cell where the cancer started.

Most cancer patients have options for their treatments. They have a few hours, a few days, or even a few months to decide and research what type of actions they would like to take for themselves. They can use their own discretion and their own cautionary measures. I, on the other hand, had thirteen hours.

I had to rely on my mother, my power of attorney, to make the toughest decisions without me. It seemed only right. She brought me into this world. I used to hear other mothers joke when I was a kid telling their children that they "brought them into this world and could easily take them out." When you're a kid and you hear something like that you believe it! You think that statement is more possible than it really is and it partially made sense at the time. My mother, on the other hand, was nothing like these mothers. She has always seen me as the greatest gift God has ever given her. She praised the ground I walked on before I even began to walk.

My mother was told while I was under that I developed SVC syndrome from the enlarged tumor. The superior vena cava is the large vein that carries the blood from your head and arms back into your heart. In this process it passes from by your thymus and lymph nodes inside your chest. My tumor was pushing on this SVC causing blood to back up in my arms, neck, and head region causing swelling allowing my mom who hadn't seen me in a week to recognize this and know instantly there was something wrong with me.

SVC is also known to cause a bluish-red color in those immediate areas affected by it. I think this would have shown up more in people not as tanned as I was. It is also known to cause trouble breathing and a change of consciousness if it affects the brain and these are both symptoms I experienced amongst many others. This syndrome alone is life threatening.

Besides this I had no other physical signs of it except bronchial cough-like symptoms with shortness of breath. The funny thing was I had always been a healthy eater and was always cautious of what I ate. Right before my California trip I weighed myself and I said to myself, "Okay, I'm probably going to eat like crap every day while I'm gone. So I'll have to remember this weight of one hundred and thirty-three so when I weigh myself when I get back I'll see what the damage is." While in California I didn't notice my body getting any bigger but I did notice my head and neck looking fuller. I joked to myself saying that I must have gained weight above the collarbone.

When I got back to California I reweighed myself, closing both eyes. I then opened one slightly while looking down at the evil machine. It stated that I lost eight whole pounds in a week. I shook my head in disbelief, got off the machine, waited, then jumped back on it again. The same number came up: 125.

I knew then that something must be terribly wrong with the machine or more likely me because I was still not feeling well. After recounting all the horrible and fatty things I ate I yet again came up with another excuse to prove to myself that I was fine and maybe this was the reason why the weight didn't stick.

I remembered that I had a hard time swallowing food and I really had to take my time and chew it up before I swallowed. I even had to take sips of water to flush it down. I thought maybe drinking more water helped along with taking my time to chew could have been the reasons I lost a bit of weight.

I don't know why I kept making excuses for myself or prolonging my misery. I just really hated going to the doctor's office and I was hoping this would just pass. So I decided to toughen up and ride it out. I never complained to anyone and I figured I must have been overworked and my body was tired. It turned out I was more right than I ever knew.

Chapter 5 - Sleep When You're Dead

I bought a ranch home when I was twenty-one years old and put a second floor addition on it two years later. So any extra money I was able to come across went directly to that. I wanted to pay off all the loans I received as fast as I could because I knew the longer I waited the more money I was going to lose due to interest rates. And I continued to pick up as many hours from all four jobs I had now at the age of twenty-five, equaling one hundred and ten hours a week. My oncologist believed this is why I became sick. I wore my body out.

I had a full-time job counseling four women with behavior issues during third shift and would pick up an average of ten hours or more a week for overtime. I also took care of a paraplegic first shift for thirty-six hours a week. I had been taking care of him since I was eighteen; he was my former stepfather.

I also worked second shift for my two other jobs that I recently acquired. One was as a tanning salon attendant. The other was as a personal care assistant for a little nine-year-old girl who had been diagnosed with Rett Syndrome at two years old. She had lost the function of her arms and ability to verbally communicate with anyone. I worked about twenty hours a week with her.

Working with her was the hardest job I ever had. I love helping and caring for others and it was killing me to see such a beautiful young girl struggle so much. She solely relied on others to feed her, bathe her, dress her, stretch her, and bring fun into her life. As a person of habit I need to see improvement in the work I do, and what made this job really hard for me was the fact that she would gradually get worse. She would eventually be subjected to a wheelchair and lose her ability to walk.

Rett Syndrome is a neurodevelopment disorder of the grey matter of the brain that almost exclusively affects females. Genetically, Rett Syndrome is caused by mutations in the gene MECP2 located on the X chromosome. It is uncommon for a male fetus to survive to full term because the disease-causing gene is on the X chromosome.

A female born with the MECP2 chromosome on one X chromosome has another X chromosome. The male with the mutation on his X chromosome doesn't have another X chromosome, but only a Y chromosome, leaving him with no normal gene. Without a normal gene he is unable to provide normal proteins to the addition of abnormal proteins caused by the mutation. He is unable to control the development of the disease causing the fetus to not develop to full term.

Females have a non-mutated X chromosome that provides them with enough protein to at least survive them to birth. The only males that survive have Klinefelter's Syndrome as well. This allows the males to have an XXY chromosome. A non-mutated X gene is necessary in order for the embryo to survive to full term. There has been as few as forty-six cases of males who have not been diagnosed with Klinefelter's Syndrome and have survived to birth, but unfortunately all have died before two years of age.

As the female infant grows, she shows all signs as a normal developing child. During six to eighteen months, she starts to show signs of regression with language and her motor skills descend. At first most parents believe this to be a form of autism until further tests reveal the hidden disorder. This is about the same time Madasyn's parents started to think something was wrong with their only daughter. She gradually stopped speaking the few basic words she learned, and as time went by she stopped feeding herself as well. They had their first child, a son Corbin, who was a few years older than Madasyn, that they used as a guide as to where Madasyn should be progressing.

After bringing their little angel to a few doctors and having many misdiagnoses, they finally brought her to one that diagnosed her with her disease. They later moved to Massachusetts because they felt that's where Madasyn would be able to receive the best care for her disorder.

I met Madasyn a year later and fell in love at first sight; like any other person who had the privilege of meeting her and her family. There staring back at me was this petite little blonde ponytailed girl with big bright eyes. Our eyes met and like a few other times in my life the world slowed down.

I felt like we were staring at each other for several minutes but it was really just a moment. She would have a whole conversation with you just using her eyes. She also did this thing to my chest that I never paid too much attention to but looking back I wonder if she was trying to tell me about the tumor in my torso. She would poke me very hard right where the tumor was. It was weird, out of character, and puzzling when she did it. It was sort of shocking and I never knew what she was trying to say.

It was winter and the holiday season was approaching us. Much like many other people I know, you find it necessary to pick up another job because what you have coming in as an income doesn't quite cover your expenses around Christmas shopping as well.

Taking care of Madasyn became my third job, bringing me to one hundred hours a week, and it was not easy work. Madasyn was a very hands-on job. It was ideal to use occupational therapy to encourage her to be more independent or improve her functional abilities, while achieving her own personal goals. As a way to communicate with Madasyn she would use eye contact with you and would blink to answer "yes" to questions at certain times.

My mother and my former stepfather Ray were together for the largest portion of my life. He taught me how to be respectful and hard-working at a very young age. Everything that came out of his mouth was a teachable moment. He wanted to shape me into an independent lady. He was also the most miserable person I have ever met besides my grandmother. He was thick-headed and always right, which was his worst and biggest characteristic. He often pushed people away. He hated his life in a wheelchair which started at the age of twenty-one. He got run over by a Springfield firetruck when they blew through a red light responding to a call and didn't see him on his motorcycle. Ray's spine was severed and his helmet was cracked into two. He was paralyzed from the waist down.

He was with my mother when I was five to sixteen. He was eight years older than my mother. He treated her as a worker and whatever she did was never enough. But he made up for it with flowers and little vacation trips throughout their travels in New England. During these travels he would bitch and complain about the handicapped rooms and things available to him.

Whenever my mother had taken enough and gave him a piece of his own medicine he would get in the car and threaten to leave us. He would take off for hours while we thought we were stranded, scrambling trying to figure out when or if he was coming back and if not what our next move would be to try and travel six hours back home. His biggest weapon against us was his threats. They came small and large. But nonetheless I loved him because he was the only father figure in my life. He said jump and I said, "how high?" I always wanted to impress him or make him proud of me. And when he wasn't that was the worst feeling in the world because he had no filter. He was good at spewing words. They were his second greatest weapon.

Looking back, I can't tell you if I was ever loved right by a man growing up. Ray was a demanding relationship and he took more than he gave most days. Our relationship was much like a game he used to play with me; the one where he would pretend to steal my nose and after a long time of whining with frustration he would only then give it back. He taunted me for his own entertainment and enjoyment most days. I was at an age where everything was literal and my heart was vulnerable.

Ray was a mechanic, one no one else could measure up to. He was a firm believer that if you want something done right you have to do it yourself. When he met my mother she was in a bad place, going through a divorce with my father. She was lost and scared and didn't know her place in the world. My mother is a beautiful woman, and I'm not just saying that because she's my mother. She was twenty-eight then and had beautiful long hair with a full can of aqua net in her teased bangs. She had shapely legs and size D breasts that complicated her hundred-pound body. Her ribcage resembled a wave to her torso. And her butt was her best feature. It was shaped like a heart. Ray was lucky to have snagged her when she was vulnerable. He's even luckier that she stayed with him for so long because, frankly, he never deserved her.

Their arrangement worked out perfectly for each other. She and I would live in our home in Springfield Monday through Friday morning. Then after school on Friday's we would venture our way to his house for two nights, then truck back to our place on Sunday night. I liked that I only had to share her on the weekends with him. I encouraged trips throughout the summer because his apartment was small and I felt out of place. I had to develop weekend friends with kids in the huge apartment complex. They were like weekend warriors. They also grew up without daddies. So we had a common anger we shared, an anger that came out when we were unsupervised. An anger that made us feel righteous when we decided to throw rocks at cars or deface property. I don't know what, where, when, or why but I learned as I grew up to stop being so angry and that's pretty much when we all stopped being close friends. Social media has informed us what each other is doing all these years later but we haven't exchanged numbers or made contact. And I am okay with that because I was my worst self when I hung out with them. I was rebellious and upset with the world. Then you throw hormones in the mix and all hell breaks loose! My pubic hair was growing as fast as my smart-ass mouth.

That smart mouth of mine had me moving out at seventeen. The biggest thing in my Italian family on both sides is respect. I don't flip my lid unless I feel like I have been "disrespected." And that particular summer day I felt like my new stepdad disrespected me. My mom had recently uprooted me from Springfield to about forty minutes away to a small town called Ware. She bought a house on Beaver Lake and my new stepdad Bob moved in with us. I had never lived with anyone but my mother my whole life and I always lived in Springfield. This was a total life changer.

He immediately started to throw his weight around and made me feel useless for housework done or not done. He looked a lot like Samuel Elliot, my mom's favorite. He also had no filter. He had potential because he was funny, could build stuff, do yard work, and, well, his dick worked. So what's not to like? Only his fresh mouth! One day he called me a douchebag in front of my mom and I lost it. No one had ever called me that in my entire life. I stood there at the end of the driveway with my mouth wide open, turned to my mom, and said, "are you really going to let him talk to me like that?" She sided with him and later suggested that if I was so unhappy maybe I should move out.

I figured this was her way of kicking me out. I took the hint. That night I packed my belongings into my backpack, a suitcase, and a duffle bag. I had her drive me to high school and never came back until eight years later when I got cancer. That was a hard time for my mother and me. There's also something else that runs in our family that most of us carry. Stubbornness. I think it stems from my grandmother who is the most miserable person I've ever met. Hate spewed from her like no other. Ironically her name was Grace. She despised my grandfather so much. She hated most of their offspring they had together.

She hated him because he never equaled up to her father who adored her and gave her the world. He also was never home because he was working eighteen-hour days to support her and

41

their five children together. Children she raised herself which made her hate him even more. It was a vicious cycle. They ended up splitting when my mother was sixteen. That same day she kicked my mother out of the house too. My mother is the middle child. Her brother Steven, younger than her by three years, and sister Julie, half her age at eight years old, stayed home. My mother grew up in a crowded household in a one-story ranch that my grandmother insisted on painting bright pink. She lived with her taunting siblings and a physically and verbally abusive mother who had many psychotic tendencies that everyone tried their whole lives to overlook.

Months shortly after, my grandfather was forced out of the house so my delusional grandmother could start dating another man. This woman, my grandmother, was abusively irrational in every way. In fact, I never heard anything good about this woman's actions except she was a great cook and tended an amazing garden. This woman complained about everything and anything and if she ran out of things to complain about she would repeat herself. She was a ticking time bomb built to destroy the lives of everyone around her. The woman simply wasn't right in the head. Her chemical genetic makeup was impaired. She thought she deserved the world and nothing pleased her. This woman should have never been able to conceive children let alone five of them.

I'm grateful that almost all of my mother's siblings were able to pick up their pieces and mold themselves into functioning, well-behaved citizens. I am also grateful that my grandmother's chemically genetic makeup was not passed down to the rest of us. My grandfather must have had amazingly strong-willed genes. God bless that man.

My mom only had one goal in life; she wanted to be a mother. She wanted to experience the bond a mother and daughter should have and be the type of mother hers was not. She is the most loving and nurturing person I know. She took care of my friends and injured animals we found in our neighborhood.

Every now and then she reminds me of how healthy she would eat when I was floating around in her womb. How she would sing to me my ABC's and count to one hundred amongst other things. She did this because she heard somewhere that this would give your child an early advantage, a head start of sorts.

She would make sure she ate one of everything from the food pyramid daily because this is what she heard the baby needed to live a long healthy life. Let's just say I was very carefully planned. She took her prenatal vitamins, took her walks, and secretly kept money stashed away for a foreseen rainy day.

She had everything covered except the right man to conceive a child with. She picked the wrong father figure, and I'm sure that's one of the most overlooked things she'll regret for the rest of her life. Maybe she always knew deep down inside she never really needed him anyway. She technically only needed his seed and once that was planted that's all she would ever need from him. Maybe he knew that too.

After I was born maybe he didn't feel needed, felt distant, and empty. Maybe that's why he felt the need to fill himself with the everlasting enchanted bottle, always chasing the bottom of every bottle filling every empty void, every bottomless pit, and every woman that would welcome him to their bed.

None of that is true. As much as I would like to try to rationalize this man's lack of fatherhood I can't and I won't. This must have been something this boy was born with, something that has stemmed from early childhood experiences.

The best decision my mother ever made was to leave this man. The second-best decision was to choose chemotherapy to help shrink my largest tumor while they kept me placed under a medically induced coma.

Without these two decisions my life would be at a loss. Maybe some of my health problems stemmed from birth. I was struggling to survive even as an embryo; that's how my mother knew I was capable of surviving the cancer because I was literally born to survive.

Unfortunately my twin wasn't so lucky. It lost its battle at the early stages of development, leaving me to survive alone. This was a huge blow to my mother. She was afraid I wouldn't be able to make it alone, that my odds were greater that way, especially because she had four miscarriages before I came around. At this point she was thinking that her only reason to live was never going to happen. Her life never had a purpose and maybe she was wrong all along.

Research has shown that in order to survive and thrive, babies need loving and caring parents. Recent studies have also shown that babies who felt loved and were close to parents in early years helped them with sickness and health later in life. Researchers concluded that parental love seems to act as a buffer against later life illness. They noticed a pattern that the loving parental relationship helps lessen the negative impact of stress and pathogens in later life. It protects the immune system and strengthens the desire to heal and live. Many studies were done by various colleges that showed students who developed cancer were more likely to have described a lack of closeness with their parents thirty to fifty years earlier.

They found that no other factor was more significantly related to illness than the degree of parental closeness. Due to new studies from all types of medical professionals, cancer has been placed under a microscope in every way possible to try and to figure out what exactly makes cancer "tick" and where it stems from. They used to view cancer as a consequence of current unhealthy behaviors, also referred to as "lifestyle diseases." Lately they've been focusing on chasing the disease a little deeper in the individual stemming back to their childhood.

While I was struggling to survive on the inside, she also had a fight of her own on the other side of the womb. My father had developed a habit. He liked to chase my mother around a room with multiple objects. My mother had to avoid bats, punches, and darts from this man. But our bond has always been about survival. Even though we had never met yet, we were one, a team, team survival.

Maybe my father sensed this bond and wanted to terminate the pregnancy. As much as I was anticipating my arrival to meet this woman who sang to me and found the time to recite to me my ABC's and 123's. I must have been skeptical of entering an unsafe world from knowing and feeling my mother's emotions. I decided to be late for my arrival. I was a late bloomer and passed my due date by almost one week. I was supposed to have been born in March but I made it right in time to be an April baby.

My mother would later tell me stories of how she hardly moved on April first so she could avoid going into labor and producing a little April Fools baby. I surely would've been picked on throughout my life with that one. But sure enough, when she thought I would never want to come out, April 3rd rolled around and I figured it was time to make my appearance.

If I avoided long odds before I could do it again. I've been doing it my whole life. This was why my mother knew I would survive my long odds with cancer, and I could pull through like all the times before.

They say a child forms a bond with the two voices they hear the most while being in the womb. My father was not the second voice I bonded with. In fact, even as a child I was weary of him. The thought of him excited me in the beginning when he would come around every once in a while. But then he kept standing me up or disappointing me to no end, so eventually I stopped looking forward to seeing him altogether. My mother never tried to shape my view of my father. She wasn't vindictive even though he probably thought she was trying to change my perspective of him like he always tried to do with me about her.

She knew over time I would be old enough to see him for who he truly was and that's what eventually happened. I didn't want to know all the gruesome details until I was a teen. It also didn't help the fact that every time I was with this man alone without a parental guardian my life was in jeopardy.

One time he fell asleep while watching me on the couch and I eventually stumbled upon a bottle of children's Vitamin C. I took the whole bottle because it had a nice orange taste to it. All of my earliest memories were times he put my life on the line because he was in a drunken stupor. I remember being in the hospital at the age of three, being extremely ill throwing up a black tar liquid. I remember thinking, *why would my mother allow me to be sick like this?* I, of course, didn't know any better

46

and all I knew was she was finally there and I didn't feel better. Another time he was screeching through the streets of Springfield in a green convertible, me riding in the center because the keg next to me took over the passenger car seat. We were cruising for a bruising with blaring sirens behind us from at least four different police cars. I remember telling my father to, "Go faster, go faster, Daddy!" For a long time I thought he got arrested that night because I asked him to go faster. As a child I felt responsible for his child-like behaviors.

I remember flailing and screaming putting up a big stink because they immediately separated us once we made it back safely to the house, which was the first time I met the chief of police. Looking back at that frightful night as an adult I can see a lot of significance in that night. My father and I shared a bond I'll always carry with me. He taught me how to live in the fast lane. My cautious mother forbade me to live that way, and because of that it intrigued me even more.

The dynamics of right and wrong will always entice me due to my genetic makeup. If my mother and stepfather didn't instill morals and ethics into me repeatedly then I may have been another wandering soul. I've never needed a father. My mother had a big enough heart, and I never knew I was missing love from another human being. For me she was enough.

Chapter 6 - A Little Positivity Goes a Long Way

When a patient finds out that they have cancer, they have to look deep within themselves to find courage. The main question is how are you going to respond and what are you going to try to do about it? Which way are you going to allow yourself to go? Are you going to be the miserable patient who grunts and moans at every little thing to no end, making everyone else as miserable as you are? Or are you going to be upbeat, bringing good energy into the room, drawing people to you, and making people want to be around you? Yup, I went with the second one too, and I was remembered by many nurses for my good attitude and they loved me. I even became Facebook friends with one of my favorites, Robin. *What a beautiful name,* I thought, for a woman who's soaring with me to help me with my health. I knew I was meant to know this woman.

Robin liked me so much she probably hoped she would never see me again. But fate couldn't keep us away from each other. I've seen her now and again and I still have that overwhelming feeling of love for her since I first laid eyes on her.

Staying focused on getting better and having a positive attitude gave me many followers and a lot of people told me that watching me struggle while still keeping a positive look on life made them stop feeling sorry for themselves about an obstacle in their life they felt was a devastating blow to their world. They realized they could have it worse and they stepped up, sucked it up, and looked to the positive in their own lives rather than the negative. Because compared to me they really didn't have it that bad.

Hope is the only thing you have to teach yourself. You have to feel it from the inside out. Without hope and faith, all of humanity would be totally lost. Pandora's Box was only able to keep one thing left inside it after she lifted the lid with curiosity and released all the evils of the world: The Spirit of Hope. It's easy to be disappointed with the cards life dealt you, but you have to keep in the back of your head that when things get rough, "this too shall pass."

The minute I woke up I wanted the tube out. The moment I was able to talk I didn't want the oxygen mask on. The minute I was able to move around I wanted to lay on my stomach, but they would not let me do this because they thought I could cut off the oxygen by having the tumor crush my trachea while I slept. I also requested my catheter out. Then as soon as I learned how to walk again, I wanted to take a shower. This was a great struggle. I must have looked like a baby calf. My legs were wobbly and I was unintentionally doing the butterfly dance. I was mortified and scared. I wasn't sure if I had to do rehabilitation and at that moment I realized I lost my freedom completely.

For some reason, it bothered me when I found out I was on the cancer floor with other cancer patients. It was the beginning of the labeling for me. I wasn't ready to be labeled a cancer patient. The idea of having cancer hadn't even soaked in yet. My identity and freedom had been ripped out from under me and I was now literally on the floor.

A part of me was still in denial. Could this really be my life now? Will I be known as the girl with cancer? Would it define who I am? Only questions were flooding my head. My brain felt like mush. Was that from the chemo? All I knew was I just wanted to get out of that room. In that room, I was April the cancer patient. Maybe if my legs got strong enough I could take a walk around the hospital gurney, IVs and all. I stirred up enough energy to make it to the door. There I could see across the hall where I saw someone that looked nothing like me, someone who was pale, puffy, old, and bald. She was the definition of cancer, or so I thought. This frightened me because in that moment I knew I too would look like that. It never occurred to me that I would look sick. I was not ready for that realization. I turned back around faster than my legs could go, threw myself in bed, and tried to turn out the lights. I asked for a Lorazepam and allowed myself to feel numb. This was a lot for a twenty-five-year-old to process.

After closing my eyes for what felt like fifteen minutes my doctor walked in. Doesn't that always happen? You could be there waiting for hours all day long for someone to talk to. And when you finally wind down and get some shut-eye, they walk in and wake you up.

The doctor addressed my concerns that there was a chance I would lose my hair, especially with the RCHOP chemotherapy because it was the strongest chemotherapy treatment available. I had tunnel vision. It made sense I always associated baldness with cancer.

Being the optimistic person I am I zeroed in on the word "chance!" Then I came up with the idea that if I didn't act as sick as the woman across the hall who lay in bed all day, then there was no way I could look as sick. And from that day forward I made sure I didn't act sick, because in my logic I never wanted to look it, and with a little help from above it worked.

Besides the common "How are you doing?" everyone usually complimented me and commented that I looked great. A lot even said I didn't look sick. I'm sure they were trying to be nice but every little bit helped. Maybe it was because I was still very dark from my San Diego trip. They associated me looking good with the chemotherapy working. I associated it with the fact that I no longer worked 110 hours a week. While I was undergoing my treatments in my free time, I calculated how many hours I would have to work, and the number blew me away. On average I worked sixteen hours a day for six months at a minimum. And if there are only twenty-four hours a day, how did I pull this off? I know I never slept eight hours at a time. My mother constantly told me I was burning my wick at both ends.

I knew she was right, but I had two sayings I liked to repeat often. One was: "Sleep when you're dead," and the other was "I would rather have all the money in the world with no time to spend it, than all the time in the world with no money to spend." Wow, that changed quickly. Now I was living life the opposite way I trained myself. I believe the value of my life went up. Now, for some reason, I'm managing my money better due to me pinching the last pennies I have. I actually have money in my savings account.

Now, I was able to have time for lengthy conversations with intellectuals on a day-to-day basis, which became one of my favorite things to do. I never had time for people before that, not outside of work that is. I lived to work. Now I got to live. The only problem was it was very hard for me to speak. The lifesaving intubation tube shoved down my throat damaged my vocal cords. I never thought I was going to recover from that.

I was not allowed to accept any flowers from people who came to visit me. In fact, when they were brought to me in the hospital, the minute they turned the corner and entered the cancer ward they were taken away and educated on the risks of what a beautiful rose and pistil could do to cancer patients on that floor. I remembered thinking that we cancer patients were really in a league of our own. We couldn't even have anything beautiful in our presence. It wasn't like I had the energy to touch them. All I had were the balloons. So many balloons. I felt like I would float away with the balloons in my room because of all the weight I had lost.

Certain factors affect the chance of recovery and treatment options. It depends on the stage of the cancer, the type of non-Hodgkin lymphoma (NHL), the patient's age, and general health. And whether the lymphoma has just been diagnosed or has come back.

There are many treatment options for NHL. But treatment options are often tailored to each patient. It depends on where the lymphoma was found to understand how to treat the patient. Lymph tissue is found throughout the body; adult NHL can begin in almost any part of the body. Cancer can spread to the liver and many other organs and tissues. NHL can occur in both adults and children. Treatment for children, however, is different than treatments for adults.

Chemotherapy attacks fast-growing cells like tumor cells. It is often very good at killing tumor cells. And it is often an important part of many NHL treatment regimens. However, chemotherapy attacks other fast-growing cells as well. So it can have related side effects such as nausea, vomiting, tiredness, and hair loss. Did you know three hundred million cells die in the human body every minute?

Finally came the day where my white blood cell counts indicated I was ready to leave the hospital. They hate telling you this but they do anyhow, the hospital is one of the worst places you can recover. Too much sickness going around leaves you unsafe. The longer you stay the more you are at risk and I was going to be neutropenic soon so I needed to get out of an area filled with sick people. Even though I got my footing back they still had to wheelchair me out due to protocol. From what I experienced I did not look like someone who was on her death bed eleven days prior. I looked skinny, tanned, and with a full head of hair. The only sign that I had to show that I was being wheeled out as a patient was my wrist band and bandages in numerous areas where I had ports, IVs, and biopsies.

I was afraid that if years were to go by I would still be seen as this cancer patient walking around with my big scar on my neck where they made the incision. I thought I may never be able to shake the cancer patient title. One look and everyone would know I was April the Cancer Girl. That would only solidify that I would never be the same or maybe seen the same. This frightened me. I had no time to prepare for this new title.

I left there with so many trinkets I must have looked clinically insane to someone who has had no experience with cancer and what it does. So many people gave me good luck coins and knick-knacks I was starting to resemble a walking Lewis and Clark drug store. These people wanted to help out in some way so they sent me trinkets, mostly religious artifacts, and the balloons! The balloons were another thing entirely. We needed extra hands from the staff just to help us carry out all the damn balloons.

My mother brought around the car and I said goodbye to my favorite nurse Robin who took the time to leave the floor and wheel me out. She said something I would never forget as she hugged me and whispered in my ear. "You are going to beat this honey, stay strong." This caused tears to trickle down both of our cheeks. I hugged her harder and thanked her so much for everything. I told her she was my angel. She nursed me back to health like a mom. I hoped I would see her again but under different circumstances, of course. *I wonder if she has a son my age,* I thought as I studied her face. She was younger than my mom. I memorized every wrinkle, every detail. Her laugh lines stood out the most, more than her bright blue eyes. She had puppy dog cheeks and auburn, brownish hair that she always kept messy. I figured this was from dedicating too much time to others and not enough time to herself which uniquely enough made her more beautiful. I blinked hard as if I took a picture of her to imprint in my memory forever. I stepped in the front seat of my mother's car and Robin shut the door behind me. That was a good moment. I am glad I took the time to capture it.

The days were coming together like a blur. I felt like the only thing I could do was sit and eat. It killed me to see my mother running around doing things non-stop for my wellbeing. She reminded me so much of what I was before this. The doctors told me that the type of cancer I had is commonly found in people in their twenties. The thought occurred to me; *would I have been off scot-free if I aged a little faster?* There were times in my recovery that I felt blessed to have certain physical and emotional characteristics that I could call mine, so I could still consider myself human.

If it wasn't one thing it was another, leaving me to disintegrate in front of the mirror or in front of others. I was starting to deflate like the balloons that were hugging the corners of my room. Looking back in old notebooks I wrote how grateful I was to still have my eyebrows fully intact as well as my taste buds. After leaving the hospital my butt was incredibly sore. I figured it was probably from all the sitting around. Heck, my ass had never seen that many chairs. I was also grateful in the beginning to still have my lingering tan and figure. I thought without this I surely looked like Smeagol.

I lost so much weight it wasn't surprising to me that the automatic sink in the public restrooms didn't pick up my motion. Was I already a ghost? Good thing they had two so I could just move to the next one and see if it also failed to recognize me. It worked and I had the courage to look at myself in the mirror. The haircut that I had gotten before I went to California now made me look like Didi Pickles from the show *Rugrats*. It looked like I could strike matches with my lips, and my skin was so ashy no Instagram filter could help me out. I looked like the black space on wide-screen movies, empty and hard to look at. But it's okay because I (mostly) don't care what people think of me. At least mosquitoes find me attractive.

While undergoing chemotherapy you have multiple stages with those twenty-one days after receiving the chemotherapy. Immediately after you feel sick for days. Nauseous, vomiting, diarrhea (if you ease up on the pain meds), and very fatigued. Then after about a week of this, the steroids start to kick in and you finally get some energy to crawl out of the bed.

Then you feel like you wasted the past week so you start to try to motivate yourself to clean the messes you made or be a productive citizen in the world again. The next stage is you becoming neutropenic. When someone is neutropenic it means their white blood cells (WBCs) are critically low that even the simplest germ could be harmful and potentially kill you. Your WBCs are like your army to fight sickness. Usually that low they are too sick to go out and do anything.

If you see someone in a public area with a mask over their mouth, chances are they are very susceptible to catching other people's germs and their immune system is critically low. Neutropenic precautions are steps you can take to prevent infections if you have moderate to severe neutropenia. Neutropenia is a condition that causes you to have low neutrophils in your blood. Neutrophils are a type of white blood cell that helps your body fight infection and bacteria.

This is the time you have to stay away from crowds and people who are sick. This will decrease your risk of infections that can be passed to you from others. You can't shake hands with anyone, share a sip of your drink, or pick up your animal's feces. You can't be around crowds and you have to avoid fresh flowers and still water. And of course, bathe daily and don't use tampons or douches. And you learn children are a walking, talking, germ fest that you need to stay clear of.

I felt like we're all running around like a rat in a cage, trying to make heads or tails of our lives, trying to find meaning or a purpose for our existence. (Notice the word "existence" has a similar appearance to the word "exit"). We're trying to find where our missing puzzle pieces fit in other people's lives. We know our species needs to procreate so we think our meaning may be found in others, so we date, we marry, and we settle down.

Thinking this is the ultimate goal or the main challenge, we rush into it because we think we're ready at the time we meet this significant other. After all, that is what is expected of us right? We learned this at an early age, the same age we learned about princes and princesses. But you were born into this world alone and you will die alone. They don't bury you with anyone. You can't take anyone with you. All you have in life is yourself and for the lucky ones your mother (like me) or a valued parent, partner, or mentor.

I feel like the mission in life is to find yourself, and that is what you were born to do. There's nothing wrong with the middle-aged man living alone across the street as long as he's content and doesn't own a set of pervert binoculars. Our planet is beginning to be overpopulated, so this procreating business is overrated. I know people like to leave something behind to be remembered by when they leave this world. If I can't have kids, then this book is my baby, hopefully.

It was hard hearing about people taking steps forward toward their future and hearing about their accomplishments while I was in limbo, waiting to see if having a life at all was in my future. I don't think anything made me sadder than this. I wasn't jealous at all but was depressed indefinitely. I hated that my life was on hold. I didn't know if I was going to move on after this or if it was indeed going to take my life. I felt embarrassed about this, and I soon started to isolate. I didn't want to talk to many people. I just let the phone ring and go to voicemail. I let my mailbox get full for many months. It seemed like everyone had some sort of life-changing great news. I was tired anyhow. The conversations would go something like this, "April, guess what? We are going to have a baby!" And then they would ask me what was new with me, and I would say, "well, the medication got me so backed up I felt like I just had a baby myself." Then the phone would go silent, and I knew I went too far as I scurried off the phone and pretended I had something to do and wasn't able to talk anymore.

Chapter 7 - Hair Today, Gone To-morrow

Just after leaving the hospital, every day seemed lost, sad, and wasted as I wasted away myself. I was constantly trying to use my counseling skills to heal myself and fight the sadness out of me. It probably would have been easier if it didn't hurt to laugh. *Since when should it hurt to laugh?* I thought. And my dreams were no help. I would have loved to have been able to escape my present reality by entering another world in dreamland. But that was not the case for me. My dreams made my sickness much more real and out of my control. All my dreams were about me being sick or recognizing that I was sick.

I had a recurring dream of being trapped in an elevator, constantly bringing me to the wrong floors, and even getting stuck in between levels.

Sometimes it was about how alone I felt. In several of my dreams, I told guy friends that I liked them, but they rejected me because I was sick and ugly. I already knew I was sick and ugly, but it was the idea of being rejected that was difficult to stomach. My subconscious stooped to an all-time low. I couldn't shake feeling sick, ugly, and rejected in my dreams or while I was awake. Why couldn't I sleep when my body was physically and emotionally drained? It was incredibly difficult living in my body all the time. I was in a constant fight for my mental and physical well-being.

I started feeling like I may never be in a relationship or be with anyone sexually again. If it did happen, it might not be for another year or so, and even then, he would have to be a strong and open-hearted person to be okay with my past. I couldn't help but wonder if a man like that even existed.

I was crushed because I secretly longed to have a companion a year before my diagnosis happened, now, I was forced into exile. That must have been where the dreams had stemmed from. I wanted a relationship because I thought it would be a great distraction from my current state. It would have kept me working toward a happier future; to live for someone other than my mother and my dog.

I began to sidetrack myself with momentary fantasy vacations that ended with the conclusion that I would die single as a bald, sick, and emotional woman. This constant inner turmoil was something I never talked about with my mother. I didn't want to worry her about my mental state because she was already having a hard time dealing with my physical struggles.

I tried to do what I could to stay positive. Most of the time, I was just staring into La La Land (yes, there is such a place). It was like my brain knew it needed to escape my body to survive. Another dream took form about me attending the Big E, a huge expo every September that sells all types of things and has famous singers, a carnival, an amusement park, and a petting zoo.

In the dream, I was there with my ex-friend Mary and Corey, my male cousin who was born three months after me. We grew up close, and I always considered him my brother. An extended cousin, Tony, was also in the dream. While at the Big E, I couldn't find Corey or Tony. I kept calling and texting Corey, and I knew he was ditching me.

I knew this dream was my fear of getting too close to Corey because I was afraid he might not be around like he was before. And I needed him now in my life more than ever. He and my friend Herald had been my rock, my mom was my backbone, and my girlfriend Mary was my anchor. I didn't know what I'd do without each of them.

Also, while in my dream, I ran into an ex. I distinctly remember telling him that nobody would be interested in a bald sick chick. A few days later I woke up, watched *V for Vendetta*, and grew balls the size of Natalie Portman's head, then asked my cousin to buzz my head.

I tried to find humor in the smallest of things. I figured, no more bad hair days, and I posted on Facebook, "Hair today gone tomorrow." I also later posted, "Now is a good time to catch lice." Running my hand through my hair was how I fell asleep for more than twenty years. I got in the habit as a kid picking out the sand on my scalp while falling asleep in the car on my way back from the beach with my mom. I still do this whenever I'm really tired and I'm trying to stay awake.

This simple pleasure had been erased. I thought, *goodbye comfort*. I woke up at 2:30 in the morning and decided after choking on yet another clump of hair on the pillow that I was ready to see it go. I thought about doing it myself like Demi Moore once did in a movie, but I soon realized I just couldn't go through it on my own.

Here are some fun facts about hair. Did you know hair will fall out faster with a person on a crash diet? Next to bone marrow, hair is the fastest growing tissue in the human body. And on average, the life span of a hair is five years.

When we buzzed my head, we were able to see how much hair I had begun to lose in such a short amount of time, only 18 days from my first round of chemotherapy. There were a lot of hidden bald spots all over my head. It resembled a globe of Earth. My mother never wanted me to shave off my hair; she thought we could work with it.

"How can you possibly think we can work with this?" I asked in frustration, as I stroked my fingers through my hair and pulled out several large chunks.

"Give me that," was all she said while snatching the clumps of hair so it wouldn't mess up her clean floors. She then ran downstairs with the hair like a bird preparing to make a nest. I never thought to ask what she planned on doing with it until I saw several bags of hair in her cellar weeks later.

She thought she could preserve it, and we could make a wig out of it. Except she soon found out you need five different people's hair to make a wig. She also cut her hair shorter than she ever had so I wouldn't feel so terrible. I think she did it to make herself feel better too.

Then I thought I might still feel pretty as long as I wore makeup every day. And this is something I began to recommend to everyone and any cancer patient. You need to keep your daily rituals no matter how much energy it takes and no matter how awful you feel. Taking a daily shower and applying the makeup you usually wear means everything to how you feel about yourself. I also recommend a few pretty dresses and a great joke book.

If you don't make yourself look presentable while already feeling crummy then you're setting yourself for a bad, depressing day. You just put together all the key ingredients to "wake up on the wrong side of the bed." So, whether you're fighting negative

62

people or cancer, I strongly suggest you go out and buy a couple of bandanas that represent you being a badass human being. I went and picked out at least 40 different bandanas that matched my outfits and dresses. I received compliments that meant the world to me at that time.

My insurance approved me to get a wig just in time for my cousin's wedding and my cancer benefit. My doctor handed me a prescription for a wig of up to five hundred dollars. After searching high and low, I fell in love with a beautiful wig that looked like Jennifer Aniston's hair from *Friends*. It somewhat resembled my own hair when it was blonde a few years before. It made me feel a little sexy. I needed that wig. My mother was willing to help with the cost because it was more than $500, and I was in a financial crisis. I had to learn all the dos and don'ts with a wig since most wigs do not come from real hair. It was all foreign to me.

After a while, the bandannas I was using would start to stink. So I would often take showers with the bandana on like my hair, then leave it to dry while wearing it. It helped keep my body temperature down. I usually washed my wig the same way. I began posting frequent pictures of me smiling looking my best on Facebook. I wanted all my friends and family to see my bravery. I also kept posting happier times I had, along with inspiring quotes that kept me strong. It was a form of therapy for me. I felt like it was the only counseling I needed. Those quotes gave me courage and hope and kept me going.

I have a strong core in me, and I believe I went into the right line of work. I knew I was a motivated person to help heal others. But I didn't know I could look deep into myself and pull out miracles for myself as well. I'm blessed to have been able to keep it together mentally while watching myself deteriorate rapidly. There are just some days and weeks you have to avoid mirrors, but you do what you have to in order to stay positive and strong. Get your mind right and avoid negativity at all costs. That stuff is toxic.

My aunt Kim planned a cancer benefit for me on June 13th. It was the most humbling day of my life. I never knew people could care that much. It was a wonderful experience to be in the same room with so many people that cared about me. I was weak, but I made my rounds. I vowed to say hello to everyone who walked through the door. To my surprise, I saw my father and two of my sisters who came with him. My father had my uncle drive him. I hadn't seen him since I was in the hospital, waking up from a coma. It was the first lucid sight I had of my mother and father being together under the same roof since I was a young girl. I snapped a picture of him "accidentally" smearing cake all over her. It was probably one of my favorite days ever. Two hundred and seventy-five people came to show their support, and it took two hours for them to call out all the raffle prizes. One of my friends, Alex, gave me his portion of the 50/50 raffle, and I cried in front of everyone with that gesture. A little positivity goes a long way.

Chapter 8 - Diamond in the Rough

Springfield is known for its blunt guts and tumble weaves. It's the city where basketball was born and has been my place of residence for nearly my whole life, except for a few years living in Holyoke (where volleyball was developed). I don't have sticky feet; I just haven't had a reason to peel myself away from here, I've never really felt the urge. Springfield has developed a bad rap as of late, but I don't feel like it's as bad as portrayed to be.

What's bad about this city is the gang violence, but they mostly just target each other. There is the occasional stray bullet, but only if you're caught at the wrong place at the wrong time, which is really only in gang territory. So my advice is to stay away from the projects and downtown, especially at night or early in the morning. Like all things bad, there are good parts too. I wouldn't trade the people I met in this city for the world, and that is probably what has kept me here for so long. I grew up in a one-family house that my great-grandfather built and lived in before my mother inherited the house. It was small and quaint and in the middle of an area that was rising in crime due to the multiple family houses built around us. When I was very young, I was not allowed to leave the yard. My house didn't have a front yard, but it did have a side lot that I was allowed to play in. The problem was that it was always overgrown with weeds. Often my mother would try to make it more playable and tend to it with Roundup, the major weed killer on the market at the time. The public still didn't know about the adverse side effects of

Roundup, and I paid a terrible price for it much later in life. But at that time, she would spray, and I would follow behind her and create my own secret garden fenced off from the rest of the world. Growing up as an only child, you have to learn to have quite an imagination even if the world is chaotic around you. This was a time in my life, just before middle school, where I was more of an introvert and tended to stay to myself. Fortunately, I took that imagination and sense of creativity with me into adulthood.

As an adult, people always asked me why I worked so much. I had a lot of responsibilities at a young age and big bills to pay. I purchased a home by myself at twenty-one and put a second-floor in-law addition on it at age twenty-two. This meant I had two mortgages, a car payment, student loans, and credit cards. I was eager to pay off as much as I could in the shortest amount of time possible. The interest rates and my second mortgage APR rates were not great.

I figured hard work would pay off later. Unfortunately, I taxed my body too much and wasn't too kind to it. No wonder it rejected me.

While going through cancer treatment, I took the punches as they came and lived my life, but I mostly just lay around. Not because I wanted to but because that's all my body would allow me to do. For months, I experienced highs and lows due to the chemotherapy and the steroids. It was like climbing stairs, and as soon as you were close to the top, there would be a strong gust of wind that knocked you back down to the bottom. It was a struggle, but I got used to the pattern.

I wanted to punch cancer in the face, but that would have been a fool's errand. Cancer could hurt me far worse than I could ever hurt it.

I learned early on that life isn't fair. So I made the best of my situation, and I wrote down my feelings, thoughts, and emotions. I didn't want to burden anyone with what was going on inside of me and make them feel more helpless than I did. My poor mother, watching her only child disintegrate right in front of her, must have been awful. I had to be courageous for her. It gave her strength. It helped us both, and it helped us both not to talk about it. I originally began to write everything down, so if something were to happen to me, she'd have that to remember me by. And she could read my thoughts when my words couldn't find the energy. I had that written on the inside cover of my first journal. I hoped it would let her know it was okay to take a peek at what was going inside of me.

I learned it was hard for people to see me like that. Withering away, bald, hunched over, unable to communicate for long periods, skinny, but resembling a balloon with eyes bulging out of my head. Because of all that, I hardly had visitors. The only time I had visitors was when they came in groups. They didn't have the strength to come alone. They needed someone to lean on or to talk to on the way here or back.

While in treatment, I realized I didn't want to be someone who became my disease. You cannot prematurely label yourself a cancer victim just because it is in the growth business. You cannot give it that much power until it has taken you over completely. Yes, they were poisoning me with exotically named chemicals, but as long as my heart was still beating, it was MY heart, not cancer's.

How come the only thing people can think to say after a tragedy is "how are you doing?" and "I'm sorry"? There should be a guidebook of things to say. I mean, I couldn't tell them that I secretly cried to myself all night until I saw the sun come up and that I didn't have to pee more than once a day because I lost all my fluids through my tear ducts. I only allowed myself to break down after I knew the rest of the world was fast asleep. And usually, the breakdown was dream-induced. I treasured these hours to myself every day. I found peace in it. The rest of the world was quiet and on the same level as me for these few hours.

I would have people coming out of the woodwork reaching out to give me environmentally friendly tips and eating tips. I got all kinds of lists from friends, family, co-workers, and passersby telling me what to eat and what not to eat based on their amateur research. I even had dozens of people telling me what could cure my cancer and what could cause it.

This is basically how it went. Stay away from non-GMOs. Stay away from sugar, "it feeds cancer." Stay away from alcohol (my least favorite thing I heard). I even have an aunt who is convinced I got cancer because I indulged in alcohol on some weekends. I guess I posted one too many times about having fun on social media. "Stay very far away from Roundup." I even had someone tell me the best way to *get* cancer is through chemotherapy treatments. I can't make this stuff up.

My doctor already gave me a list that I had to try to be conscious about. No raw eggs, which meant no chocolate chip cookie dough. No processed meats like ham and sandwich meats. Definitely no hot dogs. No soft cheese made from unpasteurized milk. Yeah…so sandwiches were out of the question. But I'm not a big Subway fan anyhow, so it wasn't a big loss. I had to double- and triple-wash my organic fruits and veggies. My mother swore up and down it was the GMOs that gave me cancer. She even protested at our local Monsanto location with a sign in her hand calling them killers. My mom is pretty badass! But the thing I missed the most was sushi. Raw seafood was another no-no. Ugh.

Doctors are never encouraged to use nutritional therapy alone. But nutrition can be a great part of a balanced treatment plan. I learned there are superfoods out there, raw honey, noni, goji, spirulina, wheatgrass, Echinacea, acai, maca powder, ginger, turmeric, raw cacao, bee pollen, durian, marine phytoplankton, just to name a few.

In fact, one of the only few choices a person has within the medical system today is what they will and won't eat. We must do everything we can to build the body up and not break it down. Stack the deck in your favor; build the immune system up nutritionally. Being malnourished cannot possibly help you with cancer.

It is illegal in most countries to treat cancer patients with nutritional therapy. The only legal treatments in these countries are surgery, radiation therapy, and chemotherapy. It is a two-billion-dollar industry that you would have to dismantle if you found an actual cure. If a cure were ever uncovered, could you imagine the effect it would have on our society?

The war against cancer has been fought with one eye closed for many years. I do not know about you, but I like to fight with both of my eyes open. People are only doing what they feel is best for them and their situation. You can be sincere, and you can be sincerely wrong. More than ten million cancer survivors live in the United States today, and three out of four families will help care for a family member with cancer. Thirty percent of females in the U.S will develop breast cancer, three out of ten! And less than one percent of Japanese get cancer, likely due to their diet.

Less than thirty percent of cancer patients survive five years after using chemotherapy, surgery, or radiation.

Now let's look at what feeds the cancer; The Olive W. Garvey Center's co-founder, Dr. Hugh Riordan, was a true scientist who believed in the power of scientific measurement over dogma. With the establishment of the Garvey Center in 1975, he routinely checked plasma vitamin C levels in chronically ill patients. He found these sick patients to be consistently low in their plasma C levels. Interestingly enough, the cancer patients he was seeing had very low vitamin C reserves. This matched scientific literature documenting low vitamin C levels in cancer patients. Cancer cells were actively taking up vitamin C in a way that depleted tissue reserves C.

PET scans are commonly ordered by oncologists to evaluate their cancer patients for metastases (cancer spread to other organs). What is actually injected into the patient at the start of the scan is radioactive glucose. Cancer cells are anaerobic obligates, which means they depend upon glucose as their primary source of metabolic fuel. Cancer cells employ transport mechanisms called glucose transporters to actively pull in glucose.

If large amounts of vitamin C are presented to cancer cells, large amounts will be absorbed. In these unusually large concentrations, the antioxidant vitamin C will start behaving as a pro-oxidant as it interacts with intracellular copper and iron. This chemical interaction produces small amounts of hydrogen peroxide.

Because cancer cells are relatively low in an intracellular antioxidant enzyme called catalase, the high dose vitamin C induction of peroxide will continue to build up until it eventually lyses the cancer cell from the inside out! This effectively makes high-dose IVC a non-toxic chemotherapeutic agent that can be given in conjunction with conventional cancer treatments. Based on the work of several vitamin C pioneers before him, Dr. Riordan was able to prove that vitamin C was selectively toxic to cancer cells if given intravenously. This research was recently reproduced and published by Dr. Mark Levine at the National Institutes of Health.

Intravenous vitamin C also does more than just kill cancer cells. It boosts immunity. It can stimulate collagen formation to help the body wall off the tumor. It inhibits hyaluronidase, an enzyme that tumors use to metastasize and invade other organs throughout the body. It induces apoptosis to help program cancer cells into dying early. It corrects the almost universal scurvy in cancer patients. Cancer patients are tired, listless, bruise easily, and have a poor appetite. These patients don't sleep well and have a low threshold for pain. This adds up to a classic picture of scurvy that generally goes unrecognized by conventional physicians. When Garvey Center cancer patients receive IVC, they report that their pain level goes down and that they are better able to tolerate their chemotherapy. These patients bounce back quicker since the IVC reduces the toxicity of the chemotherapy and radiation without compromising their cancer cell killing effects. IVC is complementary to oncologic care. IVC is not "either/or", it's a good "both/and" proposition. IVC can help cancer patients withstand the effects of their traditional therapies, heal faster, be more resilient to infection, develop a better appetite, and remain more active overall. These things promote a better response to their cancer therapy.

Research shows that the astonishingly high levels achievable only by IVC not only help fight the risk of infection and the pain of metastases, but also aid in the defeat of the cancer cells themselves through an elegant mechanism that doesn't harm healthy cells. It's a discovery that the medical world is only beginning to recognize.

Cancer is an equal opportunity offender. Having cancer is like putting a suit of armor on and bracing yourself for a battle you never signed up for. For some reason, after your first round of chemotherapy, you immediately know in your soul that nothing will ever be the same. You won't look the same. You won't act the same. You won't even taste or touch things the same. It is like all of your natural senses have abandoned you. You don't even recognize the face you've seen in the mirror all your life. Chemotherapy makes you foreign to yourself.

Once cancerous cells appear, they soon develop into a clump of tissue that lives at the expense of the entire body. This tissue crowds and wraps other tissues and cells depriving them of nourishment. Cancer grows back if you don't correct the metabolic process. If you cut the tumor out, the cells will grow back. Cancer is one of the deadliest and elusive enemies faced by mankind.

Large amounts of vitamins, vegetable juice, and organic foods can help reverse certain cancers. If you want to get rid of cancer, you must deplete your body of all the things your cancer thrives off of. High doses of nutrients can cure disease.

It is your doctor's duty to re-activate the patient's healing mechanism. If all you do is treat the symptoms, you're not going to cure the root cause of these symptoms. Taking a pill to manage an illness is not the solution to prevent the illness. There is no profit in cures. It makes a lot of sense but not a lot of dollars. Less than six percent of graduating physicians in the U.S. receive formal training in nutrition.

If you are stressed out or stressing your body, it starts to break down your vitamin C (hence the link between stress and heart attacks). That adrenaline from stress depletes the vitamin C levels in your body. The medical aspect only treats disease; they can't go back and hunt for the reason it started. There are not enough resources in prevention, and it does not keep your doctor in business. It is up to you to take care of yourself and provide nutrients to live a healthy lifestyle. You are what you eat. Heart disease and cancer are the top two killers in the United States annually.

Let's look at things organically now for a second. When you don't buy organic foods, the process can take a nutritional toll on your body. Non-organic food travels about fifteen hundred to two thousand miles and is at least a week old. What kind of nutritional value are you getting from food that's at least five days old? If you are lucky, you might only get forty percent of what you need. This food is also genetically modified, and pesticides are in everything.

Let's break down these nutrients a little more. When we cook food, we lose its enzymes. When we cook food, our immune systems react to it as a toxin, and your body goes through digestive leukocytosis. This is when you're generating white blood cell activity against the cooked food you're eating. Fifty-one percent of all your meals should be raw foods so your immune system doesn't trigger and attack any nutrients left in the food you are trying to eat.

After learning this, I have worked hard to keep fifty-one percent of my meals organically raw. These are my findings when I went searching for answers on my own. I am not encouraging anyone to steer away from their doctor's advice. He or she is the expert in your case, and I would not be here today if I didn't have chemotherapy and my mom listening to the doctors' recommendations. I'm just sharing what I've learned and what's worked for me. Hippocrates believed that the human body had an innate capacity for self-healing. He said, "Let thy food be thy medicine and thy medicine be thy food."

Chapter 9 - Side Effects

I was anxious that I would be awake for my second chemo-therapy treatment. Another round of chemotherapy meant my taste buds were going straight out the window along with my hair. But at least I still had some of my pride left. Bring it on heartburn, I'd be fully armed with a Costco-sized barrel of Tums to help me. Here I was still in the ICU on a ventilator. I was only allowed close friends and family. My mother just started joining Facebook so she could try to keep up with everyone and started a prayer group. While leaving the ICU to Oncology unit to this big hospital I was still extremely weak. When I spoke, I had to speak around an oxygen mask that drove me nuts. Most of the day I was in pain lying on my back so my mother dedicated herself as my own personal human pillow. She would plant her-self behind my back and prop me up forward when the pain got too bad.

I think it was during this time that people in the prayer group got to understand really how bad it was. She would often get messages about what they could do or provide to help her out throughout this time. She kept her requests small with the only things she thought she absolutely needed to make it through the day and to see another. Cigarettes and nips kept her right. Food was neither here nor there.

Then during my first awake chemotherapy the unthinkable happened. My mother had to run out into the hall and scream code blue for any nurse nearby to hear her.

She had seen something in me in these moments that she had never seen before. Not only in me but all of the patients she had before during her career. This totally freaked her out as she knew something was terribly wrong.

I was experiencing something called Tumor Lysis Syndrome. This occurs when the tumor releases its contents into the bloodstream as a response to the therapy. These electrolyte and metabolic disturbances can progress to clinical toxic effects, including renal insufficiency, cardiac arrhythmias, seizures, and lastly death due to multi-organ failure.

Basically, in layman's terms, when I had the chemotherapy pumping through my veins it was like a massive Pac-Man entering my body, heading to the source of the tumor and chomping at it viciously. The problem was the chunks it was breaking up were too large. My bloodstream was having a very hard time with this. I became unresponsive. I could not breathe deeply when this happened. I would lunge my hips forward as my toes curled underneath me as I arched myself backwards in a compulsive manner. To the naked eye, it looked like I was seizing. My legs would then shake out of control. It was hard to watch. Anyone that looked at me knew I needed help. No wonder my mother jumped into survivor mode as she began to panic.

All of the nurses who responded at first did not know what was happening to me. Finally one came into the room that did. She screamed out what was going on with me and everyone finally knew what to do with me.

They pumped me up with Benadryl, valium, dexamethasone, and loratadine. Thank God shortly after this experience I was finally released from the hospital. My cousin Corey followed suit and moved in with me for a short amount of time.

The next time we went to see the doctor she changed up a lot of what was going on with me from previously asked questions, going back on her knowledge and where I stood every time we turned around. Something in my mother's gut told her this was not right and this new doctor who was a previous doctor at a V.A. Maybe I didn't know what the best treatment plan for me was after all. This was going to be my first chemotherapy with my new doctor Dr. Mullally, so I didn't know what to expect. It didn't help that my other doctor had messed up on my steroid milligram dose. There was some "error" that cost me a lot of pain and suffering later down the road, with lasting effects for the rest of my life. They were supposed to prescribe me 100mg of steroids but instead, they only prescribed me 10mg. Steroids reduce inflammation, which allows your blood vessels to open and receive the full strength of the chemotherapy. That meant I wasn't able to get the best from two of my six chemotherapy treatments because my blood vessels weren't open all the way. The chemo was only working at 10% for my first dose out of six in my treatment plan. My tumor was too big to be taken down with just 10%, so we knew I was in trouble.

Luckily, my mother remembered her old colleague was now an oncologist with his own practice. She called him, and I was in his office the next day. We wouldn't have known this to be an issue if it wasn't for me desperately asking for a new prescription of liquid pain medication when in the first place I shouldn't have ran out in months to come. As I was fighting with the nurse over the phone trying to convince her how it was the best of my knowledge that I was I fact only talking 5ml only every four to six hours and it was impossible for me to have taken any more then I was prescribed because I was so very careful to not have over taken any of it due to the fear of being addicted even though it often made me sick.

She then tried telling me if I was not overusing, someone in my house was absolutely taking advantage of my stash. She then asked where I hid it, and if I hid it at all. I screamed at her with tears in my eyes over the phone that she was wrong and no one would ever do that. This ordeal had helped force my hand in changing doctors mid-treatment and if I did not have a drug-seeking family member in my house I might not be here today because that was the last straw to make my push to go with a new doctor.

I did not pursue legal action, nor will I mention the facility where this took place, but I will tell you to dot your I's, cross your T's, and do as much research as you can about your treatment. Your life depends on it. Never shut up if you think something is wrong. It's your life; the only one you have.

After filling out the proper paperwork we visited the "good ole' scale of lies." At first, I liked the scale. I had lost so much weight that I was now in my proper weight group (which I found to be totally inaccurate in today's world).

Is it just me, or are all these vintage-looking scales off by ten pounds, not in your favor? The more doctor's offices I visited, the more the nurse had to move the dial to the right. It is discouraging to see the nurse push the little dial further and further to the right. I half-wished they started from the other direction pushing it to the left instead.

Since the tumor was going to shrink, I wondered how much it weighed. Did it weigh as much as a baby? I had high hopes that when they would start to shrink it, I could drop an additional seven pounds or so.

My new doctor, Dr. Mullally, was a beautiful distraction. He was soft on my weary eyes and was the combination of all the right things, tall, dark, and handsome. But above all, he had a gorgeously sexy raspy voice.

When he gave me my PET scan results, I gripped it and held it up to my face like a baby pondering a new toy. I felt like I was looking at one of those mystery pictures where if you crossed your eyes just right, you could get a clear view of what it was. My mother was more educated on PET scan results, so I left it for her to interpret later.

This was an all-day event. The chemotherapy drip lasted for seven hours. Chemo injections feel like getting an instant bout of the flu. You feel lightheaded, nauseous, and lethargic. It's like your body knows you are pumping it with poisonous toxins and it goes into fight or flight mode. But all possibilities of flight go out the window when the Benadryl and lorazepam kick in. This is when you're lucky your mouth goes dry with fear because you'll likely drool all over yourself. Meanwhile, I found myself dozing in and out trying to watch *Lost* on my laptop. I was definitely out of it and showing signs of short-term memory loss because when I was asked a few questions, they had to ask me three times each.

I would find myself sitting in that chair for hours watching the saline drip. There was no rhyme or reason to it. Maybe my eyes were playing tricks on me, but I am pretty sure it was dripping slowly at times and fast for others. Maybe it was my mind playing tricks on me.

In one day, I spent more time around my IV pole than a stripper did hers. It had now been a month of my mother out of work and still strong by my side. She was essential to me like shoulder pads were to all her outfits in the 1980s. When you run out of strength to fight the disease, you tend to borrow the strength of others. I revered my mother.

I wished someone other than the nurses and my mother were there to talk to about receiving chemotherapy. I was receiving the harshest stuff out there and wanted to know how I was going to feel from someone else who went through it. They placed me in a private area away from everyone and everything. I assumed they did this because they didn't know how I was going to respond to it since this was the first time I was going to receive it while awake.

I later educated myself on some side effects from the Rituxan I received. This is what I read: "Side effects could lead to death, including infusion reactions, tumor lysis syndrome, which is kidney failure due to fast breakdown of cancer cells, severe skin and mouth reactions, and progressive multifocal leukoencephalopathy (a rare serious brain infection). The most common side effects of Rituxan seen in patients with non-Hodgkin's lymphoma were infusion reactions, fever chills, low white blood cells, infections, body aches, and tiredness. The most common side effect of chronic lymphocytic leukemia were infusion reactions and low white blood cells. It may also cause heart problems, kidney problems, and stomach and serious bowel problems including blockage and tears in the bowel that can sometimes lead to death."

I immediately thought of those prescription drug commercials you see on TV. They'll help your one problem but will cause you 20 others. I couldn't help but laugh out loud. What kind of roller coaster ride had I gotten myself into? *So be it*, I thought. *It is what it is*, a saying I grew to love more and more during this struggle. After all, it was all out of my control. I learned not to fret over the things I couldn't control but act upon the things I could. I took this with me for the rest of my life.

Cancer cells are acidic and immortal. They develop their own blood network to take the nourishment away from normal cells to such depth that the normal cells will kill their hosts. My body was producing cell cannibals, and the chemo was trying to reverse it. I didn't want to eat myself. Gerson said, "Chemotherapy poisons the body and kills the patient, not the cancer." He claims deficiency and toxicity are why we develop the disease. Who is Gerson? Gerson is a man who fled to the U.S. to avoid the Nazi camps and started curing people here. Nutritional therapy is a law of nature he believes in. in 1924, 450 patients were treated with the Gerson Therapy for Tuberculosis, and 446 walked away with a clean bill of health. He believed that plant-based nutrition opens up your heart arteries. After my third run-in with chemotherapy, I got a letter in the mail approving my unemployment payments. I decided this may be a good time for me to get back to my house. I had my dog, Lady, patiently awaiting my arrival. She actually wasn't patient at all. She ate my leather couch while I was away. She also ate the windowsills while she looked out waiting for me.

I needed to be on my own to fight this long battle. I couldn't have my mother or anyone else do it for me. I needed to stand on my own and relieve my roommates from taking care of everything while I was gone. My mother did not want to see me leave the hospital. I also started to take care of my stepdad on the side without getting paid for it, just to feel like I was needed. I knew that being useful would help a lot in my recovery. And I didn't know what life was like not to take care of someone. It is what I lived to do. I also knew it would get me out of the house bright and early every morning, a good start to my day.

This meant no more home-cooked meals and being spoiled with love and care every day. I was no longer tucked away in the suburbs but had time and money at my fingertips. The only thing I lacked was energy. This was a newfound freedom I had never experienced. I wanted to take advantage of it as best as I could.

I made a small bucket list of goals that I wanted to focus my time and energy on. I started with small accomplishments first. Like no more pain medication so I could drive whenever I wanted. Then find a great hiking area to take my dog so I could build endurance and muscle, get her out of the house, and spend quality time together.

My taste buds were only affected if I ate something with high sodium, but I had been craving Taco Bell for a long time. I took advantage of stopping by the drive-through on the way to the dog park. I later learned a hard lesson. While running through the woods with my dog, something didn't feel right with my stomach. It was twisting and turning, and I was in the middle of the woods with nowhere to go. It took five steps off the trail and let it loose. I had no control of my bowel movements at that point in my life.

It was humiliating. I hated having no control. I wiped myself with leaves and proceeded to jog again to try to make it to the porta-potty almost three-quarters of a mile away. A few moments later, the same terrible sensation came over me again, and I had to stop to have explosive diarrhea yet again. I found bigger leaves this time that worked better in my favor and took the chance to run to the nearest porta-potty. This time I made it and held on to the leash as my poor dog waited outside for me. After fifteen minutes I exited the porta-potty like I just left the smog from the *Labyrinth* movie. I took my time because I did not want to have an accident while driving home. Yes, that had already happened to me while fighting cancer, and I am not ashamed to admit it. It was a part of the process. After all, if crazy things like that didn't happen to me, I wouldn't have anything to write about.

Chapter 10 - Only the Good Die Young

My mother was worried about me moving back home, which was understandable. But I think it gave her comfort to know I lived with two roommates and that my immediate neighbors were extended family members my mother grew up with. My good friend Stacy's mother also lived a block away. I originally decided to buy the house I lived in to get closer to her. She was someone everyone wanted to grow to love and be nearer to. She was the most outgoing person I've ever met. Unfortunately, soon after I moved in, she moved out. But that didn't stop us from remaining close. I also took it upon myself to look after her little sister, Kristen, who still lived with her mom.

She had bought my old Mustang from me during the winter, four months before I got diagnosed. I knew how dangerous it was to drive that car during the winter, so if there were ever a bad snowstorm, I'd let her drive my new four-wheel-drive Jeep, and I would drive my old Mustang back from Texas Roadhouse where she worked.

One night, Kristen decided to go out and celebrate St. Patrick's Day with some friends. Unfortunately, she was driving while intoxicated in the last snowstorm of March. She lost control of the Mustang because her foot was stuck underneath the brake pedal, and she drove through a building, a gym called Century Fitness. She had just got done dropping one friend off and was getting ready to drop off the next. During the crash, Kristen's leg was badly cut open from the brake pedal and needed multiple surgeries to correct the severed ligaments. Her friend Britney was luckier and was released the next morning. I felt terrible for not being there. She made the newspapers, so the police had to make a big deal about it. They took her license and charged her with reckless driving. The Mustang was totaled. Her spirits were defeated.

After making the paper, her manager at the job she loved so much let her go. She obviously couldn't wait tables because her leg was in a cast, and she needed crutches to get around. She felt humiliated. She started to shut herself in and began to lose work friends after having a public argument with her boss on Facebook. She later apologized for her outburst, but he wasn't having it. After her cast came off, her self-esteem took a hit because her leg was not and would never be the same.

This little girl had more friends than I did, yet she felt isolated and alone. She obviously got grounded for drinking and driving, but even after her time was up, she wouldn't leave the house. Her mother encouraged her to go out and get a job that she could walk to, so she applied to Dunkin Donuts. But she felt like her life was going backward. What she didn't realize is that life is fickle and sometimes you have to take two steps back to move three steps forward. She went from being a bubbly, happy, beautiful girl with a fast-paced social life to a quiet girl who chopped off all her long blonde hair, stopped wearing makeup, and avoided conversations.

Her mother would spend a lot of time with her watching movies and shows on television. Whenever a funny part came on, her mother would laugh, but Kristen would show no emotion. Her mother encouraged her to get help. She wanted her Kristen back. We all did, but she said she was fine and kept dismissing the idea.

One night I was woken up by a frantic call from my girlfriend Stacy to go run over to her family's house. Her mother and stepfather went away for their one-year anniversary. In their absence, Kristen decided she was going to take her own life. Stacy told me her younger brother Patrick and her cousin Hannah, who was living with them at the time, were there and found Kristen dead.

I dropped my phone and ran out the door. Then I realized I didn't have the phone, so I had to hightail it back to my room before I ran back out down the road barefoot because my roommate parked behind me. I heard him come in about an hour before my phone went off. I ran and didn't stop until I reached her house. I saw the ambulance parked out front along with two police cars.

I turned to my right and saw the ladder leaning against the roof of her house leading into Kristen's window. Patrick was sitting on the stairs with his hands on the top of his head, staring down and away from the porch. I passed a police officer, passed the gate, and ran to Patrick and hugged him with all of my might. We sat there like that until he had found the strength to tell me what had happened and how he had found her.

I asked if she left a note. He said he didn't know and never looked. Officers were upstairs investigating the room. In between sobs, he told me that she didn't answer the door no matter how hard he banged on it. So he went into the shed, grabbed a ladder, and climbed through the window. He could hear her phone was in there because it was going off every time he tried her. After entering the dark room, he turned the light on and still couldn't find her until he opened the closet door. Due to colorization, he could tell she was un-revivable. Taking your own life is not pretty. It was not a sight a loved one should have to see, especially a brother finding his little sister like that, the girl he had always vowed to love and protect.

He got her situated and sat there powerless, too many thoughts running through his head at once. He realized he didn't have his phone and didn't think to find hers, so he unlocked the door and ran back downstairs to get his to make the necessary calls.

When someone takes their own life, it is nobody's fault. Kristen died only five months after her accident. She was attending a community college, the same one her sister and I went to. She was checking out her options for a new love life but was happy to just live without putting titles on anything. She was free-spirited like Stacy and their mother. The last time I saw Kristen was less than two weeks prior when I was at a huge luau party with Stacy. Kristen seemed to have been in the shadows of everyone else that night. She was her new distant self, and there were moments where you could see the old Kristen wanting to shine through.

I didn't know depression on a scale of that magnitude back then. Since then, I have tried to understand it. I have volunteered my time and money to suicide prevention organizations. I have walked with the families and friends of lost ones. I have cried, and I have cheered with them. But mostly, we encourage each other to pull forward and see another day.

It seems depression is everywhere; it's almost like a demon lurking behind people's eyes. It's hard living a positive lifestyle in a negative world. Sometimes it feels like the walls are closing in.

Whenever I go into a state of depression, I put my phone on silent. Sometimes my thoughts get too loud. With the select few I may want to talk to, I give them each a personalized ring tone.

When you go through something difficult, and you're having a hard time dealing with it, you want to replace that pain with something else that can alleviate or mask the hurt. Some people cut themselves, others get tattoos. I got my ear pierced along with five other awesome people in memory of Kristen Crowell. When I was ten years younger, I lost my best friend George to heart complications, so I carved a G into my ankle in remembrance of him. Ten years later, you can still see it. It's almost like life moves so fast you don't want to forget your past and the people who have affected you and changed your life. A scar can remind you of who you are and where you came from.

Chapter 11 - Triggers

Your disease wants to isolate you, to get you all alone so it can kill you. But that's not what you want. I began to ask myself if I was worthy enough to live. Most people live for orgasms and tastebuds, and I am all out of both. I didn't want people to see me bloated and bald. My eyelashes and eyebrows were almost completely gone at this point. I had nothing protecting my eyes from the stinging sweat or an errant glob of shampoo. And I still had one more round of chemotherapy left. My body was as weak as it was the day I was born.

I still can't get rid of a metallic taste in my mouth, thanks to chemo. What is it? It's the taste of your tastebuds dying. The only thing to try to get that nagging flavor out of your mouth is to suck on a salty chip for as long as you can until it turns into mush. But the metallic flavor will come back immediately, so you have to pop in the next one. There are approximately nine thousand taste buds on the tongue. By the age of sixty, most people have lost half of them. Oh, and the average person produces about 1.7 liters of saliva each day.

Chemo also caused me to develop a nasty smell in the back of my nose. A woman's sense of smell is keener than a man's. I asked Doctor Mullally about it. He said it could be the smell of my nose hairs dying. As soon as I heard that I couldn't get my hands on a mirror fast enough. Sure as shit, I had about three nose hairs left in each nostril. I know you're thinking, who cares about nose hairs? No one sees them, right? But let me tell you, they would have come in handy for my trip to Cape Cod I took later that month.

During this time, I started to get a weird sensation whenever I would dunk myself under cold water. It felt like two lightning bolt shots were running up the sides of my tongue. It was such a strange sensation. It was almost as if I had fillings that were getting shocked from chewing on tinfoil. I later found out that the tingling of the tongue is a form of paresthesia, along with burning, stinging, prickling, tickling, and the sensation of needles and pins. It's basically an alteration of our sensitivity or an abnormal sensation.

Our tongue is a highly sensitive organ as it is, rich with blood vessels and nerve endings. So any sensations like the electric shock feeling I was experiencing hint at a problem that most likely involves the tongue's sensory receptors. Medication, vitamin and mineral deficiencies, anesthesia, or other serious conditions can cause this. Not only could I not taste, but I felt like my tongue was going on strike about it. And I was right there with it in solidarity.

These are the small things you now have the time to listen to in your body. I never read the pamphlet on all the side effects chemo could give me because I didn't want to read the word "death." And I also didn't want to trick myself into experiencing more symptoms now that I would know I could experience it.

I was out on my own, taking it day by day, course by course, and symptom by symptom. And for the most part, I didn't share it with anyone but would write it down in my handy-dandy notebook.

In fact, I never researched my sickness until I was starting to write this book. I needed to apply referenced facts. The reason I never did research or tried to find home remedies is that I figured God had the ultimate decision.

After the first month, I stopped praying to God, not because I didn't believe in Him, but because who was I to say whether I lived or died? What made me so special? If standard procedure didn't work, then it was my time, and modern medicine gave me borrowed time as it is.

The best way to fight cancer is to prevent it. There is no cure for cancer. It only goes in remission. Even when I am done with my treatments, my body can still produce cancerous cells. With the stage I was diagnosed with, there is only so much I can do to try to prevent it from coming back.

Something they don't like to tell you; chemotherapy is not a cure for cancer. After coming to terms with everything, I realized life is way too short, and I need to utilize my borrowed time to the best of my ability. So I made the best out of every situation and every day.

I started working at the age of sixteen. I never had a break in my employment. This was the first time in ten years that I didn't have a job to report to. While fighting off cancer and not having to work, I was truly living for the day and in the moment. I even started volunteering for a good cause at a survival center where my friend worked.

I wanted to give back to the center and the women working there to help ease their load since most of them bought tickets to my benefit a few months back. One of these women crocheted a beautiful colorful blanket for me that I cherished dearly. I slept with it every night and brought it with me to my eight-hour chemotherapy appointments. I think it served its purpose wonderfully. It gave me comfort in a time of need.

When they hook you up to an IV and pump liquid through your veins, you actually become cold. Yes, sometimes as a patient, you can wear a sweater, but it has to be very loose so you can hike it up your arm without cutting off the circulation or compromising your IV line. And then if for some reason you get hot, you can't take that sweater off!

Here is a little tip for those of you who also hate the bone-chilling cold that eventually makes its way through your whole body (because let's face it, you can't keep the rest of your body warm if your arm is freezing cold. And the AC running like crazy in hospitals doesn't help your case either). Get some tape and two hand warmers. Place one directly where the IV line starts and one on your wrist on the other side of it.

The first thing they inject you with is saline. They call this a "saline flush." They clear out your veins first before they inject you with anything. They typically insert a 5ml syringe of saline into the medication port of the cannula's connecting hub after they initially install the cannula. If blood is left in the cannula or hub it can lead to clots forming that block the cannula. Flushing is required before a drip is connected to ensure the IV is still good.

They also flush after medications are delivered into the port to ensure all the drug is delivered fully. And they use it in between injecting multiple medications to ensure that the medications won't react to each other. This is important for complex intravenous medications such as chemotherapy.

Most people don't think about the saline flush or realize it's happening. Some people can feel the cold sensation running up their veins if the bag is not warmed.

A lot of cancer patients have triggers that make them nauseous. They are nauseous from the chemotherapy, but sometimes smelling certain things or tasting certain foods can send them over the edge and make them throw up.

You should probably stay away from your favorite foods during chemo for this reason. Besides, you typically develop a metallic taste in your mouth that won't go away for days. Metal cutlery can make the taste stronger.

One of my triggers was movement, such as long car rides. I would have to stay home on the days my nausea got really bad. Almost nothing could make me leave the house. The other trigger was the smell of saline being pushed through an IV.

I thought that was a funny trigger until I realized that my body knew if I smelled that distinct odor, it meant I would be feeling sick soon. My body associated the two, which I think was pretty smart of it.

After they inject saline into your veins, they then inject you with Benadryl. You feel it almost instantly; it puts you in a better, more relaxed state. You may think you can fall asleep too, but you never actually do because, a) you have to pee a lot, and b) you can't help but think thousands of thoughts while they are slowly poisoning you with your permission.

They told me I had young, healthy veins and did not need a port installed under my collar bone. I already had a gnarly scar at the bottom of my neck where they gave me my biopsy, so I was grateful for not needing it, especially since I can only fall asleep sleeping on my stomach. A port is a small piece of plastic or metal the size of a quarter that sits under the skin. Then a small tube resembling a catheter connects the port to a large vein, and they insert the chemotherapy with a small needle that fits right into the port. You can also have blood drawn through the port.

They keep this port in you for months until you are no longer in need of chemotherapy. They insert it only using a local anesthetic, and the whole idea of it weirded me out. I didn't like the thought of a foreign object placed under my skin for a long period of time. It was too unnatural for me to wrap my head around it. Since I had a choice, I went with the less invasive option.

But I did come into other problems because of this, as I was fixated on the chemo bag, staring at the hazardous labels on it. I noticed how cautious the nurse was being. It was as if she were afraid to puncture the bag, not moving faster than anything resembling a sloth. One drop of chemo could turn her into a ninja turtle, and that meant by the law of nature, she would have to fight bad guys in the sewer and eat only pizza for the rest of her life.

As the acid was getting distributed into my vein, I immediately knew something was wrong. An unfamiliar burning sensation began crawling up my vein. I shot my arm back, away from the sloth, and told her something was off.

She confirmed to herself that she did not like that vein. This puzzled me. Was it my vein's fault? Was it her fault? My mother then asked her how long she had been doing this, and she responded with a slothy snarl. The area around the first vein grew tender and red. My arm felt warm, and my vein looked hard and cord-like. My mother turned to me and informed me the nurse gave me phlebitis.

"What is phlebitis?" I gasped. "It sounds terrible."

"It just means your vein collapsed," my mom replied, and then stared at the Sloth with a puzzled look. "That vein is now shot for the rest of your life. And you'll have a mark there forever, like a drug addict."

I had never done drugs before, and then it hit me. I was doing drugs right now. Hence the hazardous label. From that point, I felt like maybe chemotherapy was not the answer, but I was already in it to win it and way over my head with this "treatment" plan.

So what did we do? Sloth took off talking to other nurses, blaming my vein saying I should have a port while constantly shaking her head. She disappeared for hours and never treated me again while another nurse came to my aid. My new nurse offered me ibuprofen, patched up the dirty work, gave me a cold compress to place on my arm, and attacked the other arm. If my veins gave me nine lives, I had eight more to go.

Did you know there are 100,000 miles of veins in the adult body? That is enough to circle the Earth four times. A child has about 60,000. A single vein is comprised of three layers. The tunica adventitia is the tough outer layer and is made mainly of connective tissue. The middle layer is the tunica media, which is smooth muscle with elastic fibers. The final layer is the tunica intima which comes in direct contact with blood flow. This area is made of smooth cells and has a hollow center called the lumen.

When she was done, the new nurse said, "I'll be back later. We'll see how you feel in a couple of hours, okay?"

I just nodded without understanding what could change in a couple of hours. I took out my book, *Are You There, Vodka? It's Me, Chelsea*, by Chelsea Handler. I enjoyed reading as of late because it allowed me to pop in and out of reality. I could jump between my sick world to a make-believe one, one sentence at a time.

After we were done, I was reminded by the nurses that I wasn't allowed to eat fruit seven to fourteen days after receiving the chemo. I always thought this was absurd. Isn't fruit healthy for you?

Seven to fourteen days after chemo, you get neutropenic, which makes you susceptible to infection. When I got home, I went after all the fruit in the fridge and started with the raspberries, my favorite. After digging a little deeper, I found one stray raspberry in the back that was as furry as a koala's ass. Somehow, it looked like the fur on the raspberry was moving. I instantly felt sick since I ate three handfuls while cooking dinner.

Days after the chemotherapy, I stared off at nothing all day, all the time. I would have the TV on but just stared right through it. I couldn't comprehend what the characters were saying or what the plot was. My mother would leave the room to have a smoke, then come back in and ask me what she missed. I couldn't tell her.

I asked another ex-cancer patient if they had experienced the same thing or could relate in any way. They confirmed that they had indeed experienced the same thing. They chalked it up to being a self-defense mechanism. He said he tuned things out without even knowing it.

Even now, I can get confused and indecisive. It takes me forever to respond or understand a question. It is like my brain is lagging. Like a computer that needs to dial up first before connecting to the internet.

I also tend to dwell on things, which isn't great when you're waiting around while recovering from chemo. I was doing a lot of nothing by myself. Should I have viewed it as wasting time or recharging my batteries? My energy was pretty much zapped all the time. I didn't even have enough energy to lift my head off the pillow to see who walked into my room. Sometimes, I had barely enough energy to make it to the bathroom in time. Laying down became a lifestyle... *What's that pillow? You had something to tell me? I'll be right there.* I had permanent bags under my eyes.

Chemotherapy could either kill me or the cancer. But what was worse, the cure or the disease?

Chapter 12 - It Is What It Is

I think the person who came up with "it is what it is" was most likely dying from some disease.

I liked what Paulo Coelho said. "If you live your life intensively, you experience pleasure all the time and don't feel the need for sex." Coelho wrote the best-selling novel, *The Alchemist*, which sold 35 million copies and is the most translated book in the world by a living author. Since the publication of *The Alchemist*, Coelho has produced a new book about once every two years. In a somewhat unusual scheduling ritual, he allows himself to begin the writing process for a new book only after he has found a white feather in January of an odd year. As strange as that may sound, it seems to be working. His 26 books have sold more than 65 million copies in 59 languages. "When I write a book, I write a book for myself; the reaction is up to the reader," he says. "It's not my business whether people like or dislike it." That is exactly how I feel about this book. I want to leave something behind that has my name on it to show that I actually existed. That is important to a dying person, the thought of leaving Earth faster than you were able to make a mark. We only have about seventy good quality years in us, some less than others, and that's it. If you believe in reincarnation, then you have to start all over again. I'm grateful knowing my book is on a shelf somewhere and could help someone feel less alone and empowered while going through cancer treatment.

All the pamphlets the doctors gave me told me to put on weight because it would help me beat the cancer. But, God, I hated my reflection in the mirror more that year than ever, I was hard to look at. Love thyself was definitely not an option.

My back still ached. And my cough remained, so that meant the tumor was still pressing on my bronchia cord, right? And that meant the tumor must still be large. This scared the bejesus out of me. Muggy and rainy days still make me cough. I was also bruising like a peach.

These last few months, I was in a complete daze, in a world all to myself. I never told anyone how bad it was. I didn't want them to hurt and feel hopeless in this journey. My mother would ask how I was doing all the time. But I didn't even have the energy to speak most days. Just talking took a hell of a lot out of me. Looking back now, that seems impossible because it's such an easy thing to do. But for a cancer patient, it's not. In fact, it's what most of us tend to dread, talking about important, meaningful things. If we change the subject to what's happening in the world rather than what's happening inside my body, the conversation gets even more depressing. This is the best time in your life to meditate.

I meditated all the time. I would imagine an army of white blood cells growing rapidly and spreading to another region of my body, claiming another territory. I would map out my body, and every day we would cover more ground. I would even find myself doing it in the shower. It's where I was completely alone, my personal sanctuary where I could zero in on my body both visually and mentally.

I found myself often forgetting that I had no hair and came to the realization when I took a half-dollar-sized dollop of shampoo, placed it in the palm of my hand, and smacked it on the top of my head. It would make a splat sound like bird poop. This happened to me more times than I'd care to admit.

My mom saw I needed something, so she told me if I beat this, she would take me to Hawaii all expenses paid. When I was little, she did this a lot to make up for when she wasn't around much. It would always take me out of any slump I was in. I was still stressed about the money, so she said we would stay with my uncle Tom to make it less expensive. Just two years prior, we visited my uncle Tom in Hawaii, and we loved it.

The section of Hawaii where he lived was where all the natives lived, and they disliked outsiders. They called us Haoles. *Haole* is a term used by native Hawaiians to describe people who are not descendants of native Hawaiians. It's usually used to refer to White people. In the Hawaiian language, the term has been used to refer to a foreigner or anything else introduced to the islands of foreign origin.

My uncle Tom is living out there all by himself with his books and his favorite TV show, *CSI*. He is an interesting man with many wild stories of his military days. While still in the military, he broke his footplate after jumping out of a parachute and landing on a rock. He then had to run six miles into combat. He was a sniper. Most people don't understand him, but we do, and that is all that matters. When I was a baby, I really took to him, and he was always there for me growing up. My mother's best friend was his wife at the time.

One time, he climbed up on one of my neighbor's garage roof (during one of his more limber days) and scoped out one of my mom's exes, ready to pull the trigger if he had to. Why? Because she told him her ex said he was coming over with a gun and was going to shoot her first and then himself. She always said that was more than any of her brothers would be willing to do for her.

Chapter 13 - Alien

I missed my dog Lady terribly. I hope she knew I would be back. My home was about a half-hour drive from my mother's house, and being in the car gave me motion sickness. I would often come close to throwing up. So my roommate, Judd, took care of her and my house. If it were up to me, I would have never left her side. But I wasn't strong enough to try to cook myself my own meals and clean and be human. One of the best sick days I had was when one of my dearest friends came by with my dog to surprise me. They brought their dog Dylan, who was Lady's best friend. They played in the yard hard. I think she really needed it as much as I did. It did my heart a lot of good to see her happy, running around free and loving life. It made me feel better than any medicine could.

The feeling didn't last as long as I would have hoped because they accidentally ran through the asparagus garden and pissed off my stepdad. Whenever I found myself awake in the middle of the night eating yogurt, I would instantly grow sad. I would always treat my dog to the last lick. She would wait so patiently, pleading intensely with her big eyes, fidgeting her way towards my last spoonful. She had a knack for knowing when I was at the last bite of my meals. I needed to get better for her and have a speedier recovery.

I was able to leave the house when I wasn't neutropenic, which I was very grateful for. I needed to surround myself with people who were not afraid to let loose and have fun. This helped me stay busy, positive, and enjoy the rest of what my life had to offer.

After I laid off the meds and was able to drive myself again, I decided to join my friends and buy a season pass to Six Flags. I read their quote, which was, "May the only ups and downs you experience in life be on a roller coaster." This was exactly the type of encouragement I needed. I thought, *Sign me up yesterday.*

I told my doctor about it, and he had some concerns which caught me off guard. He had advised me not to ride any rides that would instantly jolt me. He was afraid that the sixteen-centimeter tumor in my chest would dislodge and move around, causing me other serious problems. Immediately I thought of the movie, *Total Recall.* I then thought of this little alien in me moving around like that guy in the Sigourney Weaver movie *Alien.* Or from the chest of that guy in *Spaceballs* singing "Hello! Ma Baby," as he dances on the bar with his little top hat and cane kicking his feet high in the air. I decided in that moment that I should name my tumor. I first started thinking of names that go away after time, like John Stamos and Aqua Net, but I also wanted to be practical. So I just called it Alien.

Chapter 14 - Hopeful Thinking

After finding out you have cancer, you start hoping to just make it through the day. You stop asking why and start to believe maybe your sole purpose of having it was to teach you to live in the moment. You start to realize the only thing you have in life is right now. Yesterday is already gone and tomorrow isn't promised. I stopped assuming God went on His lunch break when He was concocting me and just accepted it.

You really learn how to love life again after it almost gets ripped away from you. It's like a jumpstart to your brain. You get an awareness of what it means to be alive. I found myself staring transfixed for hours just watching the canopy of leaves rustling in the wind above my head as I sat in a chair. Simple acts seemed miraculous. And with every sensation is the thought that you must have survived for a reason. You must have had a purpose to still be on this Earth. And the best part about it all is you have the rest of your life to figure it out. And trust me, you can't wait to find out what that purpose is and start your search.

It's said, "life is 10% what happens to you and 90% how you react to it." This motivated me to react with love and positive vibes. I started looking up famous movie quotes before I would watch a movie to help me understand the underlying meaning of the film. I fell in such deep love with movies this way. It's like I knew their secrets and could read between the lines. I was eager to hear these important quotes. I would find myself looking for them, waiting with anticipation while throwing handfuls of popcorn in my mouth, chewing gingerly.

This is another one that helped encourage me to push forward. "Things turn out best for those who make the best out of the way things turn out." Then I heard Captain Kirk in *Star Trek II* say, "How to deal with death is at least as important as how to deal with life." This had me thinking. Have I even dealt with the idea of my death yet? Like what is the process, the stages? How will I feel? What happens to you the minute you stop breathing? This frightened me to fight harder. I was too young to cross that path. I think it is the unknown that scares you the most. If I knew what was going to happen, it would be different. In the Bible, it says you go to sleep. So maybe I would get all the sleep I missed out on the last few years and make up for it? No, this answer wasn't good enough for me. I needed more. Why do we just sleep? The Bible says we wait to be woken up again. So we are going to be zombies like Jesus? That is even more terrifying. I never got my answers after sitting in church for half a year. I came up with a brilliant Plan A to circumvent the answers that never came, try not to die. Beginnings are scary; endings are usually sad. It's what's in the middle that counts.

Speaking of middles, after I finished my sixth round of chemotherapy, my doctor scheduled me for an important PET scan. This PET scan would tell me if I beat cancer or not. I was at a crossroads, and I didn't know where my future lay or if I was promised a future at all.

I was nervous about the PET scan, and I know a lot of other people were too. My uncle David and cousin Samantha told me to call them and let them know the results immediately after I received them.

The problem with these scans is the person on duty doing them isn't authorized to tell you how it went. So you find yourself searching deep in their eyes as if somehow it would reveal the truth to you.

The worst part about it all is waiting to hear back from your doctor. And if you have the scan on Thursday or Friday, it can take until Monday before you know the answer. That is exactly what happened to me in this case, the longest weekend of my life.

The worst was that everyone took the time to call to see where I stood. But I didn't even know. This made it impossible to take my mind off the results. At nine o'clock on Monday morning Doctor Mullally called me and told me I should come in the next day to talk about the plan of action for treatment. He informed me that the chemotherapy did not kill all my active cancer cells.

When I came to visit him, he told me it looked like the chemotherapy killed the smaller tumors in various areas of my body, but I was still lighting up in my pelvis region. This was a problem because they do not radiate multiple areas of the body; it's not protocol for my type of cancer.

I will admit, it was not the news we were planning on getting. While hearing everything, I looked over at my mother. Her wide eyes went wild with the kind of anticipation she usually reserved for the moment the dessert menu was recited to her at her favorite restaurant.

I swallowed hard to keep the vomit from coming back up. I stopped focusing on his words after a while. I zeroed in on the humming sound I heard in my ears. Her face sagged, and she looked like she aged thirty years in a six-month span.

We found ourselves gingerly searching for the corner sections of the room, avoiding eye contact at all costs; as if the answers to my future were resting there in the untouched, unlit sections.

He then told me he had already set me up with one of his colleagues at Dana Farber who could better translate my PET scans into a diagnosis.

My doctor had an excellent bedside manner. He would have to go into one room and give them bad news, then go into the next and give them good news, all while being professional and personal with every patient. He was one of my angels, and I will never forget the generous empathy he showed me.

The appointment he made me with Doctor Fisher was on Thursday. He was a very busy man who made an exception to fit me in on his lunch slot, which I was more than grateful for.

After the glass doors to his office opened, my mother patted me on my shoulder to let me know I was granted the freedom to walk out of the door.

I was told to go down the hallway, and there I would find a desk where I would wait to check out. A young woman whose name I learned the very first day but forgot immediately was there to give me an appointment card.

I looked over at the fish tank next to me. In the middle of it stood the twelve-inch Buddha I had bought my doctor weeks prior to spruce up the depressing room and bring some peace of mind to others.

I felt everything else but peace. I instantly got mad at the Buddha for trying to persuade me into being happy. I felt like there wasn't enough air in the waiting room for me. I eagerly grabbed the appointment card and nearly ran out of the office. I don't even know if I said goodbye to my doctor. Could he have approached my cancer differently so I would have a better outcome? Did they give me the right chemotherapy? I made a mental note to jump on the computer when I got home to do my own research for the first time since I found out. I put my life in his hands and trusted him completely. Should I have? Could I have done something, anything differently?

I felt compelled to yell at the strangers walking past me as they were going about their day laughing at God knows what. It felt crazy to me that the world was still orbiting around the sun, and everyone was continuing on in their day as if nothing had happened. I am not good at judging what our lives look like to normal people. Like most of the rest of the world, I wanted to be anyone else but myself.

As we were waiting for the elevator to go down to the lobby, there was an old couple ahead of us. The impatient husband kept pressing the elevator button repeatedly. I wanted to get out of there as fast as the next guy but pressing that button a hundred times wasn't going to make it come any faster. We live in a world where we want instant gratification. I gave him some angry eyebrows, and he gave me a returned look of constipation.

My mother pulled me out of my stupor. She could always make me see what was truly important even if it took me a long time on my own. And what was important was a drink of liquid courage. She always knew exactly what I needed.

My mother resembled a shark, an obligate ram ventilator, to be precise. Somewhere she lost the ability and the anatomy for buccal pumping. She needs to keep swimming, or she'll die. There are only two dozen species of these kinds of sharks out of four hundred. They even swim while sleeping. Just like a Great

White, she wouldn't exist if she didn't keep continuously pushing forward.

No matter what you do as a parent, you cannot prevent tragic events from happening to your children. There is just no way of foreseeing what can happen with them.

I hated the anticipation of this week. It may have been the worst week of my life up to that point. I kept psyching myself out. It was like my brain was battling trying to stay positive, but my mind was visiting some very dark places. I had so much hope until now. During everything I endured, I did not beat my cancer, all those sleepless nights, all the sickness, and the countless tears. The sounds of the machines humming and beeping putting me into a trance-like state. I couldn't help but think, did I endure all of that for nothing? Did it actually take more time off of my life than add to it?

Chapter 15 - Tiny Dancer

That weekend, I decided to join my friends out for a drink. It had been a while since I had more than two drinks. I had to take heartburn medicine to keep it down, but if I could get past that, I could successfully get myself drunk. I was eager to forget about losing my life's battles. I really let loose.

I wore a pair of black five-toed Vibram shoes that I loved because they looked fun. The shoes also took the focus off my looks and helped me with my balance and posture. After about four drinks, I was laughing my fears and problems away. We were outside dancing in front of my friend Eric, who was playing acoustic guitar next to a bonfire at the Waterfront in Holyoke.

It was a nice, warm night, so I wore a black dress that looked cool if you twirled me. My friend spun me in a circle, and when my right big toe caught my left heel, the rubber on the shoes stopped me, and I fell face-first on the back of a total stranger's chair.

I didn't have enough time to catch myself with my free hand and landed on my nose. I began gushing blood everywhere, and everyone rushed over to me to make sure I was okay. It didn't help that I was dancing to Elton John's "Tiny Dancer," which I requested. To add to my embarrassment, after realizing I was okay, Eric changed the lyrics to, "take a load off April." I was mortified.

Twenty minutes into blood streaming from my nose, I broke down and cried in hysterics. This made all my feelings about my sickness come up. I cried hard for a long time. And all my friends cried with me. It was sad, yet beautiful at the same time.

I told my mom what happened the next day because I didn't feel right. She urged me to go to the ER because I might need a blood transfusion. She scolded me like a child telling me I put myself in grave danger and told me why I was at such risk. On our way there, I'll never forget how hard I laughed because right after she yelled at me, she pulled over to the side of the road and stole wild purple weed roots to plant in her yard. She picked these weeds because they were purple and everything about my mother's house is purple. I found out I did not need a blood transfusion, but I did need an IV drip because I was dangerously dehydrated.

Another rare occasion where I let myself let loose a little was also in the middle of the summer during my chemo treatments. My friend Mary wanted to see a reggae band in Rhode Island, and I was definitely down for some chill vibes, especially since I was no longer neutropenic as of that week. But at that point, I didn't dare to drink. I didn't want the alcohol to work against the chemotherapy. The odds were already against me, so I decided to just smoke a little weed here and there to help keep up my appetite.

After a wonderful night out, I, of course, was the designated driver. Upon approaching the pearly gates of Burlingame Campground, I was immediately pulled over, which had never happened to me before. I felt perfectly calm because I felt I was in the right, yet I had no idea what the speed limit was, so I thought I was solid. The state trooper came to my side of the car, and I informed him that it was not my car, but I was the designated driver. He told me I was going 30 in a 20 MPH zone and then proceeded to ask me how much I drank. "Nothing," I said politely. He then asked who owned the vehicle, and I pointed to my friend Mary in the passenger seat.

He then left me alone and proceeded to walk to her side as I rolled down her window. He asked her to get out of the vehicle as he held the door open for her. It was then that he saw a sealed jar of marijuana in the door jamb where I sat just five hours ago. I had forgotten that I brought my small stash of weed with me so I could force myself to eat during dinner. He reacted as if he hit the jackpot at the casino. All I could do was sit there with my sunken eyes, my swollen face, and my wannabe Jennifer Aniston wig.

He started to chuckle. "Well, well. Whose is this?"

I explained that it was mine. He still seemed ready to reap the rewards of what he discovered until I ripped the wig off my head to show him how sick I actually was. "I am sorry, Officer, but it really helps me."

He almost stumbled backward, realizing what he was looking at, and took a minute to clear his mind.

"Just a few months ago, I wouldn't have gotten it," he said with wide eyes. "Right now, my father is going through cancer, and he has said the same thing about this stuff, so I understand. He then told Mary to get back in the car, handed her my license and her registration, and told me to slow down.

Chapter 16 - Dana Farber

At 9 a.m., we started the two-hour drive to the hospital. The waiting room at the Dana-Farber Cancer Institute was very inviting. The lights above as we walked in gave off a white halo effect. The lamps on every end table provided a yellow afterglow for the avid reader, who oddly seemed to be everywhere in the busy waiting room. I couldn't help but wonder if they were trying to distract themselves from the present situation. Even if we were the sick ones or our loved one was, we were all in trouble.

It was such a calm setting that upon second glance, I noticed people snoozing in corners. How could anyone be calm enough to fall asleep here? Every voice was soothing as if they were cooing a baby. This was exactly the environment I needed. I took a deep breath, closed my eyes, and began rubbing my bald head through my bandana. This was the only calming coping mechanism I had.

I opened my eyes, scanned the room, and realized I could distinguish the cancer patient from the loved one because every cancer patient wore comfortable shoes. I then read a quote on the wall, "Dedicated to discovery, committed to care."- Dana-Farber.

It didn't take long for them to call my name. Dr. Fisher was a nice-looking older man, salt and pepper hair, a trimmed beard, and eyes the color of the Pacific Ocean. He looked educated and respectable.

He had my chart in his left hand, then took his right hand and gave me a firm but gentle shake. I wonder if he practiced until he got it down perfectly. It said I mean business, but I am a gentle soul. It was perfect.

Sometimes when I am waiting for someone to tell me bad news, I hear ominous music playing in my head. I stiffened like a wet shirt in the winter wind. After a dramatic pause after our hello, he said he had read my chart thoroughly and believed the lighted area in my pelvis was not cancer. It was possibly the result of my endometriosis since I had just gotten my period.

Endometriosis is a genetic condition I received from my mother. Thanks, Mom. Endometriosis is when the layer of tissue that normally covers the inside of the uterus grows outside of it. It grows on the ovaries, fallopian tubes, and tissue around the uterus and ovaries. The main symptoms are chronic pelvic pain, infertility, and painful intercourse. Yep, so I also have that working against me in the fertility department. Whenever I got my period, I would be in so much pain that I felt like I was going to throw up. The discomfort was the worst when I had a bowel movement. I would shake and become clammy. My blood flow was uncontrollable, and usually the first day of my period every month, it was almost impossible for me to leave my house. I felt unable to move in certain positions as well. I dreaded when "Aunt Bertha" came around. I had been told by my gynecologist that my endometriosis is so bad, if I didn't have children in my early twenties I most likely would not be able to have any. Here I was just hardly making it to twenty-five.

So we left there empty but as content as we could be. This meant I still had a fighting chance. Now the journey with radiation would start. Just like with chemotherapy, I tried hard not to read up on it before I went through the treatment. I didn't want other people's experiences influencing my own. I was very discouraged, however.

My doctor explained that if they gave me the proper dosage of steroids after my first two rounds of chemo, I most likely would not be in the situation I was in. Even though the center of my sixteen-centimeter tumor was dead, it was the outside layer that caused concern. The outside of the tumor could influence other cells and keep reproducing. I still had a battle ahead of me.

Maybe fate was too busy killing other people that day, or the Grim Reaper lost my address? Whatever. I'll take it.

The car ride back from the doctor was a tough one. My mother and I couldn't focus on one thought to say out loud. There were a million of them going through our heads at rapid speed. I looked down at my lap and contemplated my future because nothing made sense anymore.

I remember trying to pull something out of my hat to talk about. Typically, this was an easy thing to do, but my brain was coming up empty. It was too busy filtering everything the doctor said. I would open my mouth, but nothing would come out. This can happen whenever someone experiences a tremendous amount of stress or trauma.

I recognized this feeling from past relationships or whenever I heard really bad news. Your brain is in shock, trying to process, making sure you're safe (thanks to our Paleolithic ancestors), searching for easy answers that will help you with your problem. But I didn't have easy answers. I didn't have any answers.

Hearing Dr. Fisher confirm that my only next choice was to proceed with radiation and that I wasn't a candidate for UCLA

Medical Center's radiation program was a huge blow to my strength. I was excited to get out of the state and explore new grounds, but most importantly, I was happy to only target the cells that needed the targeting without adding additional damage to my already damaged body.

The people that knew me best knew this was a sad day for me. My phone kept ringing, and I received a lot of messages, but I didn't want to talk to anyone. I just wanted to disappear.

I didn't have anything good to say. And I didn't want to relive the same conversations and negative talk over and over. If I am not strong enough to hold my tears back, then I don't want to talk. It's like feeding into the negativity, giving the cancer what it wants.

Cancer is like a bulldozer. It leaves a path of destruction, taking down everything and everyone in its path.

I learned radiation was a lose-lose situation. Either way, I was going to end up with cancer. Skip it and keep the wonderful cancer I have. Or get the radiation and have a high chance of getting either breast or lung cancer. There was also the possibility that the radiation would finish me off.

Chapter 17 - Appalachian Trail

I didn't have it in me to tell anyone the devastating news. I was so deflated. I was losing the energy to fight. I brought myself to a dark place, and I didn't know how to get out. I felt so lost. This truly sucked. All I knew was that I wanted to be as far away from my cell phone as possible. So I left it behind and headed out to hike the Appalachian Trail with my one-and-a-half-year-old yellow Lab. I needed to jumpstart my brain, and the only place I know how to do that is in the woods. If my thoughts won't take a hike, then I will!

I hated bringing my family pain and suffering. I knew I had to be strong for them.

After I packed, I made a quick call to my mother to tell her my plans. She nearly lost it. Not only did I leave it up to her to tell everyone my bad news, but I was leaving to uncharted territories alone with a low white blood cell count. Poor woman, I didn't stay on the phone with her very long. I didn't want her to talk me out of it. I think my mother knew it was something I had to do.

Just before leaving, I made a list and checked it twice. But all I really needed was my compass and a map. Sometimes you need to lose yourself to find yourself. I've always been this way. Maybe that's why I like to drink, to self-reflect. Self-reflection can come to you best when you are all alone with no outside influence. That was exactly what I needed.

At the trail, I found it difficult to leave my car and journey into the woods. If something happened to me, I was afraid someone would see it there for days and try to break in. I made a mental note of everything important in my car, and fortunately, there was nothing inside of great value. Everything was easily replaceable.

I picked a shady spot right by the entrance sign leading into the woods. I said a little prayer and hoped I wouldn't injure myself, get lost, or have my mother too worried. My trusty dog looked as eager as I felt to reach our destination.

When I got to my starting point on the trail, I began by going the wrong way. I was too busy going over the list in my head of the items I brought while adjusting my straps. After a few minutes, I took out my compass, and sure enough, I had to backtrack. I wrote in my little notebook, "Sometimes you learn you have to go south to go north."

At this point, I saw a figure coming toward me from the opposite direction. It was a transgender woman with two hiking sticks. She also wore a bandana, but it was holding back her long golden hair.

We both entered the path at the same time. It must've been fate. I would have taken a traveling companion of any kind. Actually, I take that back. I would not want to travel with a scary-looking man with rapey eyes. Yes, I had my dog, but she would just lick you to death. I did not have the fight in me, but hey, it would have been the most action I would have gotten in a while. I can't help but try to find the positive in a negative situation. Maybe that's why I got chosen for cancer?

I can't remember if we exchanged names, but I remember a lot of other things we spoke about. I let her take the lead as I followed her into the forest. I spent about an hour and a half with her talking about how silly it is to carry around a battery-operated GPS. We agreed that people should learn to use a compass and map. She said electronics dumb you down, and I totally agreed. I matched my steps with the clicking of her pole.

Oh, and I underestimated the weight of my pack. After about an hour, my back went numb.

My travel buddy expressed how her sisters were always worried for her safety and how she couldn't understand how people couldn't comprehend how streams work.

I figured since she shared a little with me, I would open up a little with her. I told her my story and why I was there. I told her I was in between treatments and that I had to undergo radiation. Funny, I couldn't tell any of my friends or family this, but I could share with a total stranger.

She had long, limber legs, and I could tell between me and my dog, we were slowing her down.

I read that in Bill Bryson's book, *A Walk in the Woods*, most hikers set a mileage goal they want to achieve. A good day's hike for a person my stature, size, and condition would be about 13.5 miles at most on medium terrain. I chose my route carefully. I didn't want to overdo it. And I wanted this experience to be fun for my dog and me. That was why I picked Upper Goose Cabin as my final destination. I wanted to sleep where other people would be near me in case of a bear attack or if Mr. Rapey Eyes was walking around.

But since I brought my dog, I couldn't sleep in a cabin. So I brought a hiker's tent.

We said our goodbyes, and I watched her go over a small hill. When I got up there myself, she was completely out of sight as if she was a ghost or an angel.

This was late summer, so all the greenery was in full bloom. I took my time taking in the canopy of trees above me. Soon, we stopped at a stream so Lady could take a sip of water. We took a left and came across several big boulders covered with moss and dew from rainfall the day before.

The only way to get to the other side was to cross over these boulders. But they were intimidating and huge. I instructed Lady to go first. I wanted to see if she could see a path I couldn't, and with skill, she jumped from boulder to boulder. She then turned around and gave me a look like, *what are you waiting for?* So I began jumping from boulder to boulder.

Then just as I thought I was getting the hang of it, I slipped on the wet moss, my left leg now pinned between two boulders. I could not touch the ground with my foot. The only thing holding the weight of me and my thirty-eight-pound pack was my boney leg stuck in place. With all the chemo I received and how fragile I was, I cannot believe my leg did not instantly snap in half. It was by the grace of God I didn't die out there alone, two hours into my hike. Thank you, baby Jesus!

Now that I was going at my own pace, I stopped along the way at times to take in the scenery. Mostly so Lady could splash in the water and drink it up. She was the type of companion I always wanted. As I hiked, fragments of memories began flashing in my mind.

It was almost as if pushing myself physically meant pushing through the loud thoughts, making room in my brain for a white static that began to creep in. It was magical and strong like my

120

steps. It was like my body's check engine light was ready to come on, but I told myself it'd be fine, and I kept driving. I was determined to complete this trip.

Then the jingle in my whistle began rocking back and forth, breaking me out of my stupor. I had it dangling from a loop on my padded shoulder strap. I needed it to call out to someone in case I was in immediate danger; it also had my compass on it. I let five minutes pass until I took it off and placed it in my pocket.

The problem with hiking with a thirty-eight-pound pack on my back was I always had to calculate my footing. It made it difficult to gaze at the beautiful landscape around me because one wrong step could take me out. I took comfort in knowing that with each step, I was one step closer to my goal. I felt grateful that my body allowed me to do this.

There was no way I could have been home another day readjusting the pillows over and over, trying to make myself more comfortable somehow. I then thought of a saying I heard once. "Nothing is ever easy except pissing in the shower." I laughed out loud and heard my voice echo on the hills around me.

Off to my left, I saw my dog play in the stream. I have never loved a companion more. She was everything I wanted and more, and I hoped I was everything for her as well.

After coming back from the Appalachian Trail, you learn to call it, "The AT" and there are only two different languages out there, the sectional hikers and the through hikers. Once you state which team you're on, you immediately get classified. I hated this. I didn't want to get classified as a sectional hiker, and if they asked me what my deal was, who I was and what I came for, I explained it was my first hike back on the trail in between treatments, with the attempt to try to gain my strength back and build some muscle. I had gained some weight from all the steroids. To be honest, this was my attempt to take charge of my own body again because I had lost control completely.

As I ran into people, I told them I came alone with my dog. I gave them my real name and explained that was indeed not my "trail name." Then I told them my trail name is Popazquat. On cue, they laughed. Instead of calling me by my trail name, they called me April. I guess that had a way of sticking with them more? I then took the initiative to introduce my dog as Lady Bird for her trail name. I always called her that for a nickname. But I suppose birds and yellow labs go together. Anyone who knew me for more than two days didn't know where I was.

I met a girl named Bea, after her grandmother, who had an adventurous spirit and who is no longer trapped in a body on this planet. She was traveling with her dad. I told her to locate me on Facebook, and maybe we can run into each other later this year or next when I gain more strength, so maybe we could hike together through a state or something. I told her I needed to build my muscles back up. She told me I was very muscular now, and she had wished she had my muscles. All the while, I was wishing I had her nice slim and petite body.

You always seem to want what you don't have. Maybe there's this magnetic energy pull that always makes you want what you don't have. Like negative and positive reactions on batteries. This has been recorded since the first humans to enter this world. Like Adam and Eve, the yin and the yang.

After that hike, one of my dreams was to be sponsored by a company to travel the full distance of the Appalachian Trail. When I came back the next day, I looked in the mirror and couldn't believe my eyes. I had to squint, but sure enough, my hair had started growing back. It was taking its time filling in around my temples. It looked silly, almost like a fade since the hair didn't like to come in on the sides. It was the softest thing I have ever touched. It was liberating, and a beautiful moment for me.

I took this as an omen that I was in charge again from here on out. I looked at myself in the mirror, and with wide eyes, I said, "I am back!" The last thing running through my brain before I fell asleep was, I probably should have named myself bald eagle. I slept soundly that night.

Chapter 18 - Radiation Consultation

About a week and a half before starting radiation, I had a strong sense of not belonging. I got in a tizzy fit with pretty much all my closest friends. I think I was pushing them away so they wouldn't feel the pain I felt. I felt antsy for the first time since the beginning of my treatment. I had this sensation that no matter where I went, I didn't belong, and I was needed somewhere else. Everything but me seemed certain of itself. I felt a sting in my soul, much like the feeling of sticking your tongue on the positive and negative charges of a nine-volt battery.

It was like I fell off track somewhere and couldn't find my way back.

Cancer had been mine and my mother's world ever since it was thrown in our laps. Somehow, it was always brought up in every conversation.

If someone asked her how her day was, her response would involve something about my treatment, my tumor, or that she was picking me up or dropping me off at the doctor's office. One time, she mentioned to a friend that she hadn't seen her in a while. The friend's response was, "Well, I just needed a break." As in, she needed a break from hearing about cancer. Yeah. Me too. My mother didn't know how to respond. She was stunned that a friend could be so cold. After a long pause, she finally said, "That must be nice."

Our grief was beyond measure, but we had an equal share in it. But it was something only I could physically hold. I selfishly took comfort in knowing I was not alone in this. We learned to pass it back and forth like riding a seesaw with our eyes closed, waiting for our emotions to shift us back and forth like a gust of wind. You have to tolerate the acceptance of suffering.

During my first radiation appointment, I met this astonishing critically intelligent seventy-three-year-old man. I could have talked to him for hours if the day was in our favor. He told me something I found funny that I would never forget.

He said he could believe that God was a bipolar woman. Maybe he was on to something. Dying people have great ideas. Cancer can be a gift because you can realize how few remaining days you have left. I tell people that I love them as much as I can now. I try to make good memories every day. Tomorrow is never promised to you. Sick patients can and should see that so clearly. And if they don't, they are likely dealing with depression and should seek help. You can choose to dwell or inspire. That's pretty much the last ounce of control you have. You can also give others strength, people you may not even know. "You only live once," but in reality, you only die once, yet you can live every day.

Memories live between synapses and between the people who carry them. There is only so much storage space on any person's hard drive. Even if you've lived a rough life, hearing the words you may die should restart your brain to want to live out the final days as best you can. Old memories can be easily replaced by newer ones. There's actually a scientific formula for this phenomenon. It is called the forgetting curve, also known as the Ebbinghaus curve.

You realize time is of the essence when you're running out of time. You can be late for something, including your funeral. You should live life one day at a time, just not necessarily in that order. You'll have a hard time coping with living if you've already prepared yourself to die. Yes, my days were numbered, but they were *my* days. Even if I didn't have the funds or energy to do anything, I would sit outside and look at the beautiful world around me and take it all in. I would listen to nature.

Staying engulfed in life even when you're dying makes a huge difference in your fight. I never let cancer break me down.

I do not want to look back and say I wish I used my time wiser. Being of service to those around you is key. When you smile, can others benefit from it? When you laugh, can others feel it? Can you look yourself into the mirror and say you are a compassionate person? If you were to leave your mark on this world, what would it say about you? How did you contribute to make the world a better place? I didn't understand the value of life until it was almost lost. The world doesn't change itself because you have cancer. Only your world does, and maybe those around you.

Sickness doesn't care if you are rich or poor; it attacks people of all ages. It is the great equalizer, and it affects everyone.

Chapter 19 - Radiation Begins

Right before my radiation started, I began to get bad back pains again. I lost my appetite, and I was tired for most, if not the entire day. I had just started working out again. It was about two and a half weeks after treatment, so naturally, it was easy for me to blame it on that. But I was secretly frightened that the tumor was starting to grow back. After many sleepless nights, I finally called my doctor. It took me going through a whole bottle of aspirin before doing so.

He was on vacation, so I had the pleasure of meeting his co-worker. She was concerned for me and thought that a new little tumor may have started to grow near my spine. So she ordered a CAT scan.

I had been through so many CAT scans in the past six months and figured I'd be getting bad news. Luckily, the following day I had my first radiation appointment, and it was standard procedure to do a CAT scan. We were able to beat two birds with one stone.

I thought that maybe the tumor was shifting my spine or was affecting my scoliosis. It could have been popping out my spine by pressing against it. Maybe my muscles in the area were not used to me exercising after so much time had lapsed. Maybe the extra weight in that region brought discomfort to the spine. The scariest question I thought of was maybe another tumor started to grow.

A while back, my doctor said there was indeed a small tumor that grew on the vertebrae but was wiped out from one of the first rounds of chemo. It didn't show up in the PET scan, and I could have had some leftover cartilage in that area that would bring discomfort to my everyday activities.

All I knew for sure was I had to constantly move around and stretch out in rotational movements. I couldn't stay in the same position very long. It felt like a constant bruise to the touch. The only thing that would give me any relief was a deep tissue massage that my poor mother had to apply. I could feel the liquids inside me move around. My back had a mind of its own, and a voice too. It would snap, crackle, and pop whenever it wanted.

I was scared about getting radiation. It seemed to kill people. I was about to be lying down through a radiation treatment, not knowing at all what was happening to me. I told myself I could just rest and sleep through it since I would be in a dark room. I could imagine a laser pointer aiming toward my chest, picking off every cancer cell like an army of snipers taking out their prey.

I wasn't sure what to expect during my first appointment with my new radiologist. I then realized I was only there for her to discuss the procedure. She explained that all the doctors who had their heads in my folder thought that the risks of not receiving the radiation outweighed the risks of going through with it.

She also had me sign a waiver form that makes the most comfortable people uncomfortable. I was now basically signing my life away. I had to acknowledge that I understood the possible risks and the potential benefits, along with the possible side effects. Did I really have much of an option? I gave my consent without a moment of hesitation.

I found out that they were radiating a large portion of my chest, my clavicle to my collarbone. This would affect many cells, organs, and tissue. Yes, it would help kill the cancer, but it would also kill, destroy, and damage many other things in its path.

I started to get nervous about what this would mean for my future, if I had a future. With chemotherapy, I would have two weeks off after an eight-hour treatment to allow my body to recover and produce new red blood cells. I learned the standard procedure for radiation is numerous treatments within a six-to-eight-week period. I was in for the entire eight weeks.

After the CAT scan came back, it revealed no new tumors were created or pressing on my spine. Nobody tells you cancer is supposed to hurt. So if you need a bit of Tylenol or pain medication to get you through the day, then do it. I always thought pain medication was bad for you and could cause other issues such as addiction, dependency, and constipation, so I tried my best to stay clear of them. But because of that, I suffered. I just wanted to get off all the medications and start feeling like myself again. I didn't want drugs to take control of my body. Pain makes you know you are alive, right?

I went back for my second appointment with my radiologist so they could tattoo me. They have to do this precisely in the area that needed treatment. This was my second tattoo, so I made a joke about it. After learning the news, I asked them which one was the tattoo artist, and this time was it free. Well, free for me anyhow. The tattoo is permanent so it can always be used as a waypoint for future health care providers.

If I were ever at risk for cancer again, it would leave a map. The tattoo is a black dot; a period placed at the center of my chest, a little off to my right. The "tattoo artist" uses a sterilized needle to implant a small amount of ink under the skin.

I was told it would feel like a bee sting, and that was a pretty accurate description. It was much less painful than having blood drawn. It resembled a piece of dirt smaller than a freckle.

Chapter 20 - Tattoo Brothers for Life

I started to write because I heard how much it helped my friend Mary and her mother, the wife of a great man who lost his battle to lung cancer.

They, unfortunately, discovered the cancer too late. He left behind a journal for them to read. In it, he shared his thoughts and experiences with cancer. While I was escaping death for the time being, I decided I would leave something for my mother to read in case I didn't make it. I wasn't sure how much time I had on my hands, and I wanted to leave her some words of comfort.

She loved me before I was born. The idea of having me was often what kept her going. Being a mother was the one accomplishment she always wanted. I knew this, and I knew my sickness was killing her too.

I could picture her excited to flip through each page. She always told me if something were to ever happen to me, she wouldn't be too far behind. These words were like the news of a prison sentence being delivered, continuously echoing in my head. It worried me to my core that she might take her own life after my passing. So I made sure my expiration date never happened.

My old friend's father was excited to go home and show off his first tattoo. Unfortunately, he did not beat his cancer. I was the last person to speak with him.

I came over to visit them after hearing he wasn't doing too well.

His wife suggested I go hang out with him by the fireplace. I hadn't seen him in five weeks, and I was eager to see how he was doing. I couldn't believe my eyes. He was in the living room shriveled up on an old love seat that looked like it wasn't providing too much comfort. He had a blanket over him, but it was thin, and I could see he lost a lot of weight. His eyes and his cheeks were sunken in, and I was nervous he would see me gasp at the sight of him.

I remembered thinking, *thank God he's sleeping.* I pulled up a chair and sat close to him.

His eyes flickered open slightly as the shadow from the fire next to him danced across his face. It was a surreal moment. I took his hand and spoke softly. I wanted to bring him comfort. He had lost all muscle mass, and his chest bones were so exposed, I could fit my fingers in between them. His body was giving up. It was clear he was losing his battle, but I didn't want to discourage him, so I said the only thing I could.

I told him he needed to fight and beat this, how much he was loved by his family, and how much they needed him. He moved his fingers in my hand and said, "I know, I will." Then his breathing became shallow, and his body went limp. If I had a blood pressure machine with me, it would have told me he was dying.

He never spent any time in the hospital. He passed away peacefully early the next morning where he wanted to be. I heard it was a beautiful moment. Our conversation was the last one he had.

For some reason, I associated dying from cancer with losing weight. He was a thin man before he underwent treatment, and he didn't have any extra fat to lose. He never had a chance to finish his radiation treatments after his chemotherapy. He was diagnosed as stage three, and the doctors were optimistic that he would survive. As I sat next to him in February, holding his hand and telling him to fight, I didn't know a storm was brewing inside of me as well. A storm that I would also have to fight because I had people who needed me as well.

I had lost a lot of weight before my cancer was discovered than when they placed me in a medically induced coma. I lost even more because I did not get a feeding tube.

So, remembering how he looked, I searched for the same signs within me once I was able to walk to the mirror. I think he helped me fight because I knew I needed as much nutrition and food I could get my hands on. Whenever I was too nauseous to eat, a picture would flash in my head of him, and I would eat a second helping. Whenever my terrible thrush took over my mouth and throat, I would shovel in food past the sores and burning sensation. Oh, and it also feels worse when you smoke.

I noticed I was not gaining any weight eating two helpings of the same plate around dinner time, so I knew I needed to switch it up. I wasn't eating because it tasted good; I was eating for survival. My tastebuds died off after the first application of chemotherapy.

This is when I started to eat a whole bag of chips in a day for the fat and because chips would eliminate the lingering metallic taste in my mouth. Right before bed every night, I would have a huge helping of a dessert, topped off with a heaping mound of Cool Whip.

I finally started to see the scale climb with these last tricks I discovered. My face still looked swollen while the rest of me was slowly catching up. I later read that it was normal for patients with non-Hodgkin's lymphoma to have swollen faces. Six months after my chemo started, I saw that my face was finally starting to decrease and go back to normal.

I chalked it up to gravity, and all the fluid was starting to drop to form a double chin. My mom said my face was probably going to look like that for a while until the tumor blocking the blood to my head shrunk a bit more.

Chapter 21 - Pain Lets You Know You're Alive

After my first application of radiation, I noticed a change in my body. With chemotherapy, I had a lot of energy due to the steroids, but my brain lagged. Now my body was lagging, and my brain was awake.

It felt so good to just go home and rest after radiation. I was lucky that I did not have to work at the same time I was getting treatments.

I had to drive an hour away to get treatments. I had decided to go home to my dog that literally ate my leather couch due to her separation anxiety only a few months earlier. I felt good, then I felt better. I didn't anticipate the radiation would knock me down so low. I should have gone back to my mother's house, but I needed to be with my dog, so I felt conflicted.

After only two applications, the radiation had taken a toll on my body. I had to nap after I got home and go to bed early. It was like the excitement in me had vanished into thin air.

I had written in my journal that it felt like the radiation machine withdraws energy from you and sucks the life out of you. I felt depleted and defeated.

I would try to drink a Red Bull or a coffee, and it would have no effect. I started to lose my appetite. I would eat before going in and not eat again before I eventually fell asleep.

I often fell asleep around dinner time, but I didn't mind because I had no ambition to cook and was frequently experiencing diarrhea and sometimes throwing up.

Fridays were a lifesaver. I couldn't wait to have a two-day break from actively killing myself with a radiation machine. I started to feel like a cancer patient again, one that would soon require help. I learned to speak up after I lost a substantial amount of weight. I knew I couldn't keep doing it alone, but I was too proud to go back to my mom's house. Especially since I was finally able to be on my own again only two months earlier.

I learned when people around you offer to help carry your load, take it and simply smile and say thank you! It doesn't make you a weaker person if you just ask. Sometimes you have to put your superhero cape in the wash. At The beginning of treatment, take note of the people who offer to help you. Write it down in case you get chemo brain like I did. Then put those numbers and names on a list and store it in a safe place.

This is why it is a good idea to stay connected to others through social media or a family member who can speak on your behalf.

When I first started to walk again, my legs vibrated like loose exhaust pipes. But I had family and friends who were there to help me walk to the bathroom. These are the anchors in your life.

They will not forget to offer you help again when they know you need it. Sometimes people are bound together by tragedy. Pro-tip, I would not contact someone who was in your life a long time ago. There was a reason they are no longer in your life. Maybe they were unreliable or brought stress to you.

It is very important to live in a stress-free environment when fighting cancer. Bills and other stressors should take a back seat to what is important, your health. There will always be another bill, but your days are numbered. We have learned if you are worried about future bills coming in, ask your nurse to give you the contact information for your assigned social worker. This can help you out in great lengths to guide you to the next steps that can help you gain some control back of your financial status.

My mortgage company stood by me, as did other companies to whom I owed money. Even if it was only thirty days, thirty days meant everything. In thirty days, I would have more answers, what my chances were, and where my health would be.

Sally Mae, however, did not budge. I don't know if everyone we spoke to never heard of cancer before or if they just didn't care. Time and again, they kept putting me on hold to speak to someone else. And there is nothing like being on hold when you have cancer. Cancer doesn't hold.

Everyone kept saying, "We loaned her money, and she said she was going to pay it back, so now we need her to pay it back." It put a lot of pressure on me until my mother said something to the last guy before she hung up on him, and it made complete sense. She told him, "Since you people can't come up with a solution for her, we are just going to have to set your bill aside and give you nothing because you cannot get blood from a stone." And just like that, she hung up the phone.

She told me to just worry about surviving because that is what is most important. That I shouldn't worry about my credit because it would have to go to collections for a long time before anything could be done about it. And if I passed away, they wouldn't be getting a cent anyhow. There is always an underlying current; I called mine "bills." I had two homes, one where my mom was and the other where my bills arrived.

You can almost hear sucking sounds when the bills would come in the mail. Sally Mae was like a tree that wouldn't bend but wanted paper from another. Maybe planking started from trees. Unfortunately for them, they were not as important as my mortgage.

One time, they called me and heard my mother's TV in the background and snickered that I could still pay my cable bill. How typical. I was so pissed, I hung up. I didn't have the fight in me. After a while, I just let my phone ring. My voicemail was full, and it got to the point where I just kept my box full. I finally answered one day and told them I was dying. Finally, someone on the other end actually cared. She said she put a note on my case and said I shouldn't be getting these calls every day anymore. I thanked her profusely, and we hung up.

The weather started getting cooler, so I could start bringing my pup to my radiation appointments with me and have her wait in the car. The appointment would usually be about 20-30 minutes.

While lying flat on the radiation table, as stiff and still as I could be, I couldn't help but think that this was like lying in a coffin. That terrified me. It made me change my mind to be cremated after I died.

My body also hurt from having to lie so still. I wish I saw a massage therapist, but I have a hard time letting people put their hands on me. But I highly suggest massage therapy for others going through this.

Bringing her helped me greatly. I knew I would never let myself get in a car accident if she was in the car with me. Highway driving is always so mundane to me. I was a little worried that if I had to respond and act swiftly to something like a hard break or an accident, my body wouldn't respond fast enough.

But with her, I could never let that happen. It wasn't even an option. I would try to exercise with her by my house on the way home to try to stretch my legs. I would go to the dog park. I found it comforting going there because people were in and out all day coming and going with their busy lifestyles. That time of year, it was even more packed with people. It brought me comfort because if I were to faint or collapse somewhere on the trail, I knew it wouldn't be long before someone would find me.

I got very weak. There was a period where I didn't even have the energy to do much of anything, including write. Then I couldn't find any pens. When I found the energy to track down a pen, I couldn't find any paper. I never used to like to listen to my body when it told me to rest. Now I have no choice.

Chapter 22 - Depression is Not a Side Effect of Cancer; It's a Side Effect of Dying

While battling cancer and going through treatment, my behavior started to change. I now found that being in crowded places to be incredibly difficult. I got self-conscious and doubted who I was and what I represented. For the first time in my life, I couldn't wait to lay low during the winter months. I felt like a phony if I put the wig on. I felt like it was obvious I was wearing fake hair, and that the wig was getting tattered and loose on me. I was afraid someone was going to bump into me and knock it off my head. I had to start wearing a headband to keep it on my head tighter. I no longer had an eyelash to bat. And I felt guilty for falsifying my looks, as if I was being deceiving. I also discovered that people are nicer to you if you wear a bandana rather than a blonde wig.

My bald head was like a magnet. It attracted so many stares. Whenever I met new people, I started by exposing the elephant in the room, my health. I could tell people were curious about my health based on how I looked. Whenever I did this, more people would find a way to join in the conversation and tell me how they knew someone who had cancer, like their aunt's sister's friend. It was as if this somehow made them an expert on cancer or if they were a part of some cool and exclusive club. But trust me, this is not a club you want to be a member of.

I would instantly feel bad for that aunt's sister's friend. This woman never knew she was going to be a topic of conversation anytime someone said the word "cancer" somewhere. At one point, I realized I was that aunt's sister's friend.

And to some, I was an open wound to people just by my appearance. I reminded them of those they loved, lost, or who were currently struggling with cancer. At times, I would have to kindly excuse myself and ask where the restroom was. I learned that my sanity isn't important to anyone else but me. Never give someone a piece of you who doesn't deserve it.

This was one of the biggest reasons I stayed single during my treatments. I had to live a carefree lifestyle, and men in my past had only complicated my life or gave me grief.

Don't get me wrong, there was nothing I wanted more than to find love before I died like every other sappy cancer movie, but I was supposed to live a stress-free environment. and I didn't want a man to be a literal nail in my coffin.

Another thing I had a hard time with was second-guessing if people really wanted to be around me since I was always available. Would they want me around now that I was the vulnerable one at less than my usual best?

It was my biggest insecurity at the time. I didn't know my own value sometimes and often underestimated myself. I needed to continue working on finding myself, the biggest goal in all of our lives.

Being stuck with myself for long periods without anything to do was eating away at me. And I was only comfortable around certain people; only with those who were around when I was first diagnosed. I felt comfort in them always being there for me.

Everyone saw me starting to struggle, and I began pushing people away. In my mind, if I did not beat this thing, it would be easier on them. Right or wrong, at the time, it was a way for me to be in control, especially because I felt so out of control due to the cancer.

I was depressed. Some people go to support groups to counteract their difficulties or depression. In my case, I felt like a support group would make me more depressed. There is nothing they could say that wouldn't cause me to look around the room and feel awful for everyone, including myself.

Did you know that one out of fifteen people will actually make it to see old age? Cancer can be a chronic disease or a fatal one. There are over six million ways you can die each day. So be thankful you made it through another day.

I was told I should go see a counselor. I couldn't do that because I used to be a counselor. I felt like everything I needed to hear was already inside me. I just had to reach inside myself and pull it out. My support system found comfort in knowing that at least I was writing. It was my way of coping.

The idea of turning my journals into a book didn't cross my mind until I was done writing my third journal. I only told a select few at first.

I knew I had a chance to be an author after I found out Social Security Disability picked me up for at least three years.

It gave me great comfort thinking that this book could help other people going through the same emotional or physical difficulties. I must have carried this burden, and what better way than to turn it into a gift for others?

Many people have a diagnosable mental disorder. Some barely touch it, and some are in the greatest denial. More than two-thirds of people who have a mental disorder are in denial, don't want to admit it because they think they're flawed, or remain silent because of stigma.

Chemotherapy can cause chemical imbalances, so if you don't feel like yourself, that's okay. It is hard to feel like you when there is a battle going on inside of you.

If you have lashed out at a loved one, reconcile with them. Tell them a lot is going on you aren't in control of right now. If you are not patient, it's hard to understand. Ask your doctor about some literature or pamphlets that you can pass along to your co-workers, friends, family, and neighbors. Everyone you meet may not know what you are going through. But cancer has a ripple effect.

Cancer is one of those words that everybody knows but doesn't fully understand unless they have walked in those heavy shoes.

Just don't forget to take a deep breath in and say to yourself, "This too shall pass." And if someone in your life expects you to be your old self while you are going through this whole ordeal, then they have unrealistic expectations.

Just remember to forgive each other. If need be, reminisce with photos to see what life was like before your diagnosis. Make goals of things you want to do together once the treatments are over with. But always make memories in between.

You learn that what drives you is different than what makes you happy. Sometimes the things that make you happy are the easiest. Some people refer to it as "the little things." Keep doing the little things. The little things can take you a long way. It is not about how fast you get to the finish line; it's how you spend your time before you get there.

Chapter 23 - The Human Body is a Complicated Thing

At first, when I told people I had cancer, it was like living my worst day over and over again. Like the movie *Groundhog Day* but with higher stakes and a lot less Bill Murray.

They always asked the question, "How did you know you had cancer?" This is such a reactive question, like they were afraid they were showing symptoms that made them question if they also had cancer. This is probably how AIDS victims may have felt back in the 1980s.

Some ask questions as if they could catch cancer from you or could educate themselves in that moment on how they could possibly prevent it. As if I had all the answers. The truth is, I thought of myself as the picture of perfect health until I got sick. Everything changed after my diagnosis, and not for the better.

Maybe I got sick because I isolated myself too much with work? You already know I have always had a strong work ethic. There is such a thing as chronic social isolation, which seems to be permanently damaging for all kinds of animals. Cells taken from animals that have undergone chronic social isolation grow differently.

The cells themselves change their structure and function. Instead of making neurons, these stem cells make more of the same isolated stem cells. Spending a lot of time alone isolated from others is also known to change the chemical makeup in your brain.

I remember feeling lost and alone as the tumor was growing to the size of a plum. Embracing the isolation because I felt I had no other choice caused me to develop a bit of anxiety and paranoia. I thought it was because of my lack of sleep, not because I had a monster growing in my chest draining me of my life force.

I ate infrequently and fought my body that demanded sleep. In my isolation and busy work schedule, I started to resent my life and I stopped liking myself. But I kept telling myself (as always) if I worked my butt off at an early age while I had the energy, it would pay off when I got older.

The human body is a complicated thing. God created such a beautifully complex specimen. Humans are the most successful bacteria alive.

With all humans, it's easy to lose ourselves in superficial differences like appearances or beliefs. At the end of the day, we all want instant gratification, no matter the cost. And we try to make ourselves and our wants the center of the universe. But the truth is, our lives are universally insignificant. Our world is like a bubble ready to pop.

The closer you are to dying, the more alive you become. So alive I became.

My close friend Chris took me to the beach in Wellfleet on the Cape and let me stay at his friend Kate's beach house. He went above and beyond to make sure this was going to be a weekend I would never forget. We crammed in so many first experiences and fun that it truly was unforgettable. When we arrived, we headed right to the beach. He heard about how I got a free surfboard, so he was eager to teach me. We loaded up the boards, wetsuits, bathing suits, and a few beverages and met up with a couple of his surfer friends.

The water at the Cape is absolutely freezing, maybe the coldest I've ever experienced. It also did not help that my body was so vulnerable. I told him I didn't think I could fully submerge, so he advised me to pee in the wet suit he lent me for the day. I looked at him like, *really? That's your solution?* For the record, it did work, but only briefly. Like less than a minute briefly, but it was enough to give me the courage to go out there. I mean, I couldn't just pee in this dude's wet suit and then turn around and go back to the beach…could I?

He then began to go over the basics. It was more complicated than people think. The only way you're getting on top of your board and surfing a wave is if all the stars are aligned. Everything has to be done perfectly for it all to work out in your favor. Which, for me, it was not. Besides the lack of muscle due to my physical limitations from cancer, I also lacked *nose hairs!* Every time I would try to tread water, without fail, I got large amounts of ocean water up my nose and down my throat. This suffering lasted about forty-five minutes. I pressed on until I almost threw up water. I was practically drinking it straight out of the ocean. I then washed up on the shore like a dead seal 100 yards away from where my blanket laid and fell over heaving. I wasn't disappointed about my performance or lack thereof. But I was mortified to find out I lost my bandana in the ocean. It didn't help that the bystanders rooting me on were all handsome men who saw me at my weakest. I never got back in the water that day with my board or any day after that. Surfing just sort of leaves a bitter taste in my mouth. So yes, nose hair can be important!

I also found the hair in your ears is very important. I had water trapped in both of my ears. I kept yelling, "I can't hear you." They then showed me a trick. If I jumped up and down a few times, the water would naturally fall out. It worked like a charm since I had no hair trapping the water in. This little experience made me realize it is close to impossible to learn to surf while undergoing chemotherapy and losing all of your hair. First, having no eyebrows leaves you vulnerable to getting water directly in your eyes. Second, having no nose hairs doesn't prevent water from splashing up your nose, choking you, and making you swallow it. Third, you won't be able to hear the instructions on how to surf because your ears are almost immediately clogged.

I decided my tan could use a little upkeep, so I started to apply the lotion I bought when my friend Chris told me, "I love tanning lotion. It smells like strippers." He always had a knack for knowing how to make me laugh when I needed it. This is probably why I decided to take this trip in the first place.

After we left the beach, we picked up some lobsters and champagne (my two favorite flavors together) and eagerly cooked them up. Next, Kate had a little surprise for us. She called for a limousine to take us to sing karaoke. She knew I had never done karaoke, so they wanted to scratch that one off my bucket list.

I hadn't had much alcohol since my whole ordeal with cancer started. For one, the heartburn would get bad. Alcohol would irritate my mouth sores. And I didn't need it while I was fighting for my life. But this was a special occasion, and I needed that good old liquid courage. Except there wasn't enough liquid courage in the world to get me to sing karaoke on that stage alone, so I had my good friend Chris get up there and help me be brave.

He picked the song, and I sang my heart out. I even jumped up on a table and danced until it fell over, and I almost broke myself. I am a hoot when I drink, and I really needed this.

Chris was right, he gave me a weekend I would never forget.

Chapter 24 - Spiritual Guidance

I did not grow up in a religious household. Both of my grand-parents believed in God and brought that belief to the rest of us. They believed in a higher power that loved you unconditionally. One who sacrificed His only Son for you and your sins. That is what we learned to believe. When I was in first and second grade, I had a hard time with religion.

Something was happening to me, and I had no answers as to what it was. My mother is a very spiritual person who caught onto something happening to me when I was young, and I remember it well. When I was a kid, I claimed I saw spirits. As I grew older, I used to ask the other kids about their experiences with spirits, and they looked at me like I had nine eyes. They made fun of me and threw me out of their circles. I didn't understand at a young age that this is something you don't talk about. History is full of people becoming outcasts because they were different. We still do this to each other.

I went from group to group to group in middle school until I was left alone and felt like a monster. My mother told me it could have been because my twin passed away, but that didn't make sense. It made it worse. These spirits were distracting, and I felt so alone. I even stayed back in second grade and then trans-ferred to a different school. I jumped around a lot in middle school. I transferred four times in that small amount of time.

I would also have ESP dreams. I would only see death and tragedy. I would know something bad would happen before it did. One night, I woke up crying. My mother heard me, and I told her I had seen a little girl drown in a lake somewhere, and we had to save her. We had to let her know what was going to happen to her before it was too late. "Honey, that could be anywhere in the world," my mom replied.

That was hard to hear, so I said, "Well, why is God showing me these horrible things if I can't help and do something about it?"

She said she didn't know so I started to scream, cry, and curse God for doing this to me. I told Him if he considered this a gift, he could take it back. I didn't want it anymore.

After that night, I had somehow closed that haunted door. If I allow myself, which I don't, I can have a sixth sense. Though things happen in twos for me with my dreams. After I would have the dream, it would come true in two days, two weeks, or two months. Two Sundays later, on the front page of the newspaper, was a story of a little girl who drowned in the lake while saving her older brother. I freaked out and cursed God again.

Certain premonitions have happened since then, but nothing as memorable as that. It depends on how "open" I am. I guess you can say I haven't had the greatest rapport with God, but I always thought He was there and could hear me. I asked Him to forgive me for that night I yelled at Him.

Later, while going through cancer treatment, I made a pact with God that He couldn't take me yet because I still hadn't fallen in love. I believed that's where my search was going to lead me. Even though when you have cancer, you are loved more than you have ever been. Even acquaintances give you strength due to the love and aura they send your way.

Chapter 25 – Emotionally Constipated

In the midst of everything, I decided to sign back onto a dating website. My old profile still existed but was deactivated. The old me, with vibrant smile and long brown hair was there staring back at me. It was hard to look at those last few pictures I took before I got sick. I deleted them. I had to replace them with the new me, the short-haired blonde with sunken cheekbones and wild eyes. I looked like a completely different person.

I had to change everything on the "about me" page too. I was nothing like I used to be. I used to be ambitious and career-oriented. I used to be so future-driven. I had everything. The job, house, the dog, the white picket fence; the only thing missing was the man. Hence why I put up a profile, to begin with.

I sat there conflicted and confused on what I should write for my new profile. How could I describe why I was unemployed and had all this time on my hands? There was even a section on there about if I wanted children. There wasn't an option on the list for "cannot have."

It took me days to finally complete my profile and be comfortable with the amount of information I put on there. I just grazed the surface with who I was now versus who I used to be.

When I first found out I was sick, all I kept thinking about was, "I can't go yet. I've never fallen in love. I've never been married. And I never had any children."

I missed out on a big chunk of life that I hadn't yet been able to experience. This saddened me like nothing else. Before I got the all-clear of cancer from the doctors, I used my free time to start to try to date again. I believed with everything in me that I was going to kick cancer's ass, so I started to plan my future again. I wanted all the things I felt I was missing so I did what every other single person does in the 21st century. I went on a dating site. Plenty of Fish to be exact. I mean, it's not like I was going to meet someone in a store or bar who would say to themselves, "Wow, look at that beautiful bald girl. I wonder what her name is."

So I took a bunch of cute pictures of myself in different angles in different places with hats on, looking thin, and with makeup, and it seemed to do the trick. I had guys interested and my personality did the rest. After talking to certain people for a lengthy bit of time and they started to see I wasn't such a bad person, I would open up and let them know about my medical history; then we would agree to meet. All the back and forth kept me pretty busy. I went after the hot ones because I wanted a beautiful baby boy. It was what I always secretly wanted, a beautiful little guy I could call mine.

After a few phone calls, I weaned out the "good" from the "bad." One guy sounded like he was an old man living in the woods, misguiding as many bewildered campers as he could to his cabin. It was super creepy. Block, delete, next.

The first guy I met in person was completely wrong for me. I took one look at him and knew I would be in trouble. He was tall, had ocean blue eyes, blonde hair, and looked like he lifted weights in his sleep. He had womanizer and "himbo" written all over him. It was my fault for not screening him well enough because I was too busy messaging two other guys at the same time. He looked like a one-night stand kind of guy, the STI chlamydia but in human form. I wanted a father in my imaginary future child's life.

Oh man, how do I get out of this one? I thought. This guy had the biggest ego I had ever seen. And something else bothered me about him. He was a huge muscular man with little hands.

So what was I going to do? I could drink a bunch of beer on this date and gas him out. But I left my vanishing smoke act at home. Should I keep the date going and continue to listen to how wonderful he is? Should I allow him to kiss me, so I could say at least I got to kiss someone? Nah, he probably had herpes too, and man, I just went through a body cleanse with chemotherapy I was not going to contaminate it so soon.

I decided to go with the sick card. The food I ordered happened to be too spicy, and spicy stuff now made me cough, so I listened to my body on this one. A cough releases an explosive charge of air that moves at a speed of sixty miles per hour. Nothing is funnier than seeing food fly out of your mouth and onto your date's plate during a coughing fit. He was disgusted, and I was laughing my ass off in between lung spasms. It was by far one of my proudest moments where my mind and my body were in sync. That did the job. He was horrified. Thank goodness he was more than halfway done with his meal. After that date, he didn't contact me again, and I was grateful. I may have ruined it for any other sick girls out there. If so, you're welcome.

Then there was another guy we'll call Johnson. Johnson and I met the same way I met Mr. Chlamydia, through a dating site.

Johnson was a cop, and we had a lot in common. Since I had a criminal justice degree, we had a lot to talk about. This lasted weeks until we finally met. He worked late hours, so I only got to see him after the sun went to sleep. He was my make-believe vampire boyfriend. After three weeks and a bunch of dates later, I started to invite him to my house. I wasn't renting out the extra room in my house, so we had the place to ourselves, and he was great with my dog.

One night, I decided to let my guard down, and I drank a bunch of liquid courage. We ended up taking the party to my spare bedroom, where the door shut all the way, and I didn't have to worry about my dog barging in or getting dog fur stuck to our clothes or skin. I was mentally ready to take it to the next level with Johnson. He was hot, had a huge owl chest tattoo, and we shared some of the same ethnic backgrounds so our future child would be beautiful. Plus, it had been over a year since I had been intimate with anyone. We very gingerly took each other's clothes off until we were down to our skivvies.

It was getting hot and heavy, and I had an inventory of sexual supplies next to the bed. I reached down to touch his actual Johnson, and I broke my nail. I kid you not. I pulled my hand back from under his tent and looked at my finger as I said out loud, "Shit, I broke my nail."

"How did you do that?" he asked.

"On yo dick!" I laughed so hard I snorted because for once in my life, I spoke without filtering myself.

I went in for round two. This time I was able to understand what I was working with. He was *hung*. Like it was so big you could see it on Google Earth. I knew it was over before it started. There was *no* way that thing was going to fit, and if it did, at some point, it would change and alter me forever. I was crushed. So I did what any other lame girl would do. I gave him a hand job. My upbeat mood changed drastically, poor guy. A girl with Parkinson's disease would beat the hand job I gave him. I don't think I have to tell you either one of us called each other again after that night.

One of the things they give you before you leave the hospital as a cancer patient is pamphlets, lots and lots of pamphlets. One of these pamphlets had big text on the front, "Sexuality and Cancer." I laughed when they gave it to me, but I was starting to think maybe I should get around to opening that bad boy after all. I had all the pamphlets stacked neatly next to my bed along with the numerology book that I bought, looking to find answers about my life. Don't judge me. When you get a cancer diagnosis, you'll look for answers, and you won't care where they come from.

So I flipped through a pamphlet that started out with, "Chemotherapy and Sexual Desire." It basically stated the obvious about losing your sexual desire and chemotherapy giving you physical effects that make you feel like doggy do-do, leaving you with little energy for a relationship. And let's face it, folks, relationships are already hard work! It did say something that sounded promising, however. "Sexual desire most often returns when a woman feels better." I was then referred to jump to page thirty-two with the headline, "Ways of Dealing with Sexual Problems." After my little fiasco last night, I nearly choked on my coffee as I read, "What to expect: When you first think of restarting sexual activity, you may be afraid it will be painful or that you will never reach orgasm again. Your first sessions of love-making may not be what you expected." I started to laugh out loud.

I then met someone else who was my first Asian-sensation experience. I figured, hey, he can't be packing like that last guy! If I were to listen to stereotypes, this could work in my favor. My closest friends met him and nicknamed him "Sparky" since he was an electrician on the side. He also had beautiful freckles! I thought I died and went to heaven. I kept waiting for the other shoe to drop as to why this guy couldn't be mine. He had his own house that he built himself. He had quads, kayaks, and made good money. He lost his father to cancer, so he knew a bit of what I was going through. He also had a twelve-year-old child and was divorced for eight years. I had him over for a little get-together with some friends, and I could tell he was feeling out of place. He was six years older than me. I didn't care; I thought he was an oldie but goodie. Unfortunately, the age gap showed when I had a room full of friends who were much younger. We had some fun dates, went to a comedy show, went quadding at night, and spent the day at Bass Pro Shops, which was like a Heaven on Earth. We had a blast together, but something just seemed off. But we continued to date for three months. I still couldn't feel any emotional connection to him. In some ways, he was what I was looking for. I said I wanted a husband that goes to work clean and comes back dirty.

Maybe I just needed to keep men at arm's length for the time being. I wouldn't want to croak on anyone just yet. So I became attracted only to men in different area codes. I'd held my emotions in for so long it would have taken a saint to pull them out of me. I did what any other dumb girl would do, I let Sparky go. Pinpointing where you're supposed to be at any given time in life is impossible. You don't have a life GPS. Doing one thing takes away from doing ten others. Yes, you create your own future, but you sure as hell miss out on a lot of other paths as well. But whenever you may be, someone is missing out on the experience of being with you. You will always be missed.

Who knows if there is actually a blueprint out there with your name on it like Sylvia Brown says? I decided to put dating in the rearview for at least six more months. But I couldn't help myself and I went outside my area code again where I found "The Biker." He was boxy-shaped and had this devilishly mean look to him that I found attractive. *This is a guy I'm going to have a lot of fun with*, I thought to myself. And I did.

My hair had grown in some, so I dyed it blonde and kept it short and curly. I bought a leather jacket, wore high boots, and almost changed my name to something spunkier. I jumped in his world, full force. He was fascinated with religious artifacts of all kinds, which intrigued me more. He traveled either by his Harley or a big black monster Jeep he put a lift kit on that he called his "Big Bitch." He was a beer-slinging, no job, bad boy. God, what was I thinking? I was going for the bad boy look, I guess, and I found him. Maybe I wanted to find someone where I knew it wouldn't go anywhere, afraid that my body was going to remember it was supposed to expire. So I just had fun with it. That lasted three seasons. We had fun but he wasn't trustworthy, and already living in a different area code.

In a way, you want to destroy yourself before your body self-destructs on you. You give up on soul searching. I was never able to go out drinking while being sick. I didn't want to contaminate my body and stop the full effect the chemotherapy could have on me. So I didn't drink for most of the year. But I made up for it for the following year with him. That's when I learned the best how to live for the moment and not the future.

My mom was so good and understanding about the whole thing, too. I'm sure it was hard for her to sit back and watch me go through this "destructive phase." All I know is, what I had been doing wasn't working anymore and I needed a release. I needed to be around someone who didn't know me as the sick girl. I yearned for it. I was over the label, and I demanded my body back.

I grabbed my beer bottle like I was choking the life out of it. One drink to remember and one drink to forget. There's always a deeper wound somewhere if you look for it. I was trying to bury mine. I jumped out of my area code and into his. I could now understand why people just pick up and leave all their friends and family behind. I guess you could say I was having an identity crisis, and that was okay with me. Every hangover begins with taking inventory and ambition, and back then, I always had both. After about a month of encouraging liquid at a local bar, I finally turned to him and said, "Did you drink enough to want to come back to my place?" We were inseparable for the next four months.

I knew he wasn't my "one." He couldn't find my g-spot if he had a handheld GPS. And I heard somewhere that's how you knew you found "the one." Maybe I dated him because I was closer to menopause than puberty. Our relationship probably made as much sense as Larry the Cable Guy getting his own show on the History Channel.

I once heard a saying around this time, "He who makes a beast of himself gets rid of the pain." I was in beast mode. The world has a way of distracting you when you need a distraction.

It was kind of like swimming in waves and getting thrashed about off course.

Finally, after waking up with a splitting headache, I went to the bathroom to check out the damage. On the sink, I noticed our toothbrushes were kissing, and I had to break it up. I wanted out before this bad boy could fall in love with me; it would be a recipe for disaster. Lucky for me, he was piss-poor and couldn't even afford the gas to get to me, so my phone took the beating.

I later made a fire in my front lawn and sat beside it by myself, staring at the flames. It was October, so it was getting colder. But I didn't mind. I felt numb anyhow, both mentally and physically. My mind and body, both compromised, contorted like a pretzel. I couldn't tear my eyes away from the flames. Beautiful things can be mixed with treacherous things.

It was like God was painting with his big box of crayons again, or the little demons dancing in circles were demanding my attention to acknowledge their presence. I couldn't peel my eyes away from this transfixed state I was in. I stayed that way for close to two hours. Until the logs went cold, or the demons moved on to their next victim. I wondered if this is how the embers felt.

Chapter 26 - Floridan Slip

My father remarried when I was about eight years old. He had three more girls, the oldest being eight years younger than me and the youngest being fifteen years younger than me. Almost immediately, he moved to another state two hours away. Whenever I saw them, I never treated them like my half-sisters. To me, they were my sisters. From the time I was fourteen to eighteen, my father was doing well. Unfortunately, that was the only time I got to see my sisters, when I was invited to their birthday parties.

One year, my stepmom threw me a birthday party. I think it was the year she married my dad, and she wanted to impress him and show she could be a good stepmother. So she went all-out. All I remember is I really wanted my real mother there, and I was sad she wasn't. I never received anything for my birthday from my dad and stepmom after that. Not even a phone call. This was also about the time my dad tried to entice me to say bad things about my mother so he could try to get custody of me and no longer pay child support. I remember this trip because it stood out more than the others. He had actually picked me up from my house, which he never did. And the whole ride back, I remember I felt so loved by him for taking the time to come and get me that I was willing to do anything and say anything he wanted. I just wanted him to know how much I loved him back. I didn't know this was all a ploy to tape-record me and then play it in court when he filed for custody a week later.

I kept forgiving him and giving him more chances right up to the very end. I think I was his biggest regret, and maybe he was mine. Unfortunately, my sisters and I grew apart as strangers due to everything.

My stepmom would mail me pictures here and there when the girls were little. They had matching outfits every time. I was glad my father settled down with a woman who could keep him on track, for the most part. Unfortunately, like all good things, they do not always last. He fell off track due to his substance abuse addictions.

I couldn't help thinking about the power of good and evil. Being a psych major, I learned a lot about psychological disorders and how quickly our society wants to label people and send them down the pharmaceutical path to self-revelation and sometimes destruction. I once wondered if Jesus were alive today, would he have ended up in a mental institution? This saddened me to the bone.

While trying to date and going through cancer treatment, I had one incredibly busy week where I got multiple intense phone calls. One was from my friend Justin living in Tampa. He wanted to see if I was going to make it to his wedding the following weekend. I told him I couldn't confirm just yet, and I would have to look at my financial situation, which was the truth. I blew a lot of money on Mr. Wrong and our wild adventures, and I knew I would be losing my unemployment any week now. I pondered the idea, and a little sun would do me good. My cousin Michael, who also lives in Florida, had asked me to come and meet his two-month-old second baby girl in Fort Myers. I took my ritual nap and slept on it some more until I got a phone call from my aunt Yolanda, my father's sister. She called to regretfully tell me my grandmother had passed away the night before.

I was never very close to my grandmother. I remember going there often as a child playing with my younger cousin Melissa who was raised by her. Whenever my strongly accented grandmother would talk to me, I hardly understood her. I just nodded my head like the obedient child I was raised to be and guessed at whatever she was saying. My go-to responses were to either be more quiet or see if food was ready.

As soon as I was entering my teens, my cousin and I got into some innocent trouble. The parents did what parents do and took sides and chose to separate us for some time to see if there would be a tipping point where one child blossomed and the other one didn't. In my heart, I never forgave my grandmother for this because I had a deep love and appreciation for my cousin. In fact, I felt that way about all of them since I grew up as an only child. At that time, my cousin was the closest thing I had to a sibling.

Some chapters in your life end with not much notice or reasoning. Unfortunately, that chapter closed for me. We never rekindled what we once had. We had different groups of friends, different schools, and as fate took its course, different futures. Eventually, everyone in my father's family was a distant memory except my aunt Yolanda and her daughter Nicole.

My grandfather passed away six years before my grandmother and his last breath was the first step in her deterioration. She lost her identity the minute he lost his. It was sad to hear about her decline during those last past years. They moved to Kissimmee, Florida, when I was starting to hit puberty. So that helped put a wedge between our relationship as well. My grandfather was

100% Puerto Rican so I couldn't understand him either, but he loved me nonetheless. I was the perfect little blonde hair blue-eyed girl he always hoped for in a grandchild. I guess they are in high demand in Puerto Rico. He adored me, and I adored him right back.

One year before they left for Florida, my grandfather retired from the Ludlow Correctional Facility as a corrections officer. When you think about it, what a terrible waste of life it is to work your butt off for forty years, then shrivel up and die to be nothing more than a distant memory for another forty. Maybe it was easier to exist like the pioneers did. I guess with everything there are the pros and cons; like they often died from diseases that can now be cured with tiny pills. There were no expectations back then beyond simply staying alive and keeping your family safe. People must have loved hard back then. Especially since there were no social norms or media and all they had was one another to count on and cherish.

I thought about all of this as I laid there waiting for the flooded gates to open up and hit me. Nothing happened. Was I as dead inside as the tumor was? What was wrong with me? I decided I needed to re-find myself. I was going to Florida to attend my grandmother's funeral, see my cousin's new baby, and attend that wedding. I took my phone out from under the covers, plugged in my flight search, and spent the last arm and a leg I had making my way to Florida with a rental car waiting for me in Tampa. The wedding would be my last stop, so I figured it would be the best place to start.

I arrived at the airport and went downstairs to the rental car dealership. I partied a little too hard the night before with my girlfriend Amy and left my ID in her wallet since I never usually bring a purse. So, no big deal, right? I had my passport. Wrong. The car dealership refused to honor my rental agreement because I needed my license. Luckily, I had Amy overnight me my ID. I had no choice but to call my buddy Justin.

The conversation went like this. *Hey, it's me. I'm a dumbass and forgot my ID back in Massachusetts. I know I am not supposed to see you until next weekend, but can you pick me up from the airport tonight? And can you let me crash and then bring me back in the morning? Also, what is your address so my friend can overnight my ID?*

Thankfully, he came through.

This was the first time I met his future wife. She was polite, considerate, and quiet, everything he wasn't. I tried studying them that night, trying to find out how their relationship worked. Guy meets girl. Girl likes guy. Guy moves in. Girl falls in love. Guy asks her to marry him. Is that all it took? Maybe it was the simplicity of their lifestyle I thought as I looked around to their rented condo. White walls, the color was already picked out for them, so they didn't have to agree on that. There was nothing on the walls since you couldn't put holes in them. No need to shop for appliances since they were already provided.

I pondered all this and noticed each of their sections of the house. God bless my friend, but he will always have Hulk Hogan on the best wall of where he lives, and she complied.

They were generous hosts and offered me a stiff drink before I fell asleep. As this was happening, I saw a little sparkle in my friend's eye. He knew after seeing me that if everyone who he invited to his wedding was actually going to show, it was going to be one giant shit show. The type that always went down when we got together. For as long as we knew each other, we would always try to one-up the other.

We would go to bars and create totally different identities, accents, jobs, names, whatever came to our psychotic brains influenced by alcohol. We would separate than run back into each other with our new diverse personalities with a member of the opposite sex by our side, waiting for the next line of bullshit we were willing to offer. Looking back, I think we did it for ourselves and not for them. It was for our own amusement.

Justin and I met when I was working at a mall kiosk called Body Jewelry for You. He had these gauged horseshoe earrings that constantly found a way of losing their balls. I saw him at least once a week. He was my best customer at three dollars a ball. After about a month, I started feeling bad for him, so I did a buy-two-get-one-free deal. Shortly after that, we exchanged numbers and partied hard. After all, I just turned twenty-one, so I was open to suggestions. We hung out religiously every other weekend for the next two years while he attended Westfield State and I at STCC for criminal justice.

And at the end of the week, we always had one hell of a story. We were both the only child in our families, so maybe that had a lot to do with our crazy personalities.

I woke up disoriented, not realizing where I was until I saw that same stupid Hulk Hogan artifact. Then it all came together. This damn cat took over the couch all night. *Evil things*, I thought as I sat up. *I wonder how much of my soul that thing took away.* I stood up and started for the bathroom. Where the hell is the porcelain goddess? For my first attempt, I walked into the closet. The week was not starting the way I had hoped.

Two attempts later, I sat on the cleanest toilet Justin ever owned. Well, that was a bonus to this whole marriage shenanigans. As I sat there contemplating the pros and cons of a marriage, I got walked in on mid-stream. Damn, they forgot I was here already. Now that his future wife saw me half-naked up close and personal, and we were basically blood brothers for life, I had to accept her into my life. It didn't help that I was afraid she would tell everyone what I looked like indisposed. I shimmied my pants back up, and before I knew it, the time had passed, and I was already in the rental car on my way to my cousin's to see the new baby Olivia.

She was more beautiful in person than in her pictures. My mother's families always made beautiful babies with blonde hair, blue eyes, and skin the color of sand. I was always the darkest one out of the bunch with my skin color due to my father's ethnicity thrown in the gene pool. Because of that, when I was younger, I saw myself as the black sheep, but I guess most kids think that way.

I could tell she was happy to see me too because as soon as I got to hold her, she projectile-vomited all over me. I swear some breast milk got in my mouth. I played it cool even though I was screaming on the inside. I just ingested two different people's DNA at the same time, a first. I do a pretty good job of keeping my own DNA down and to myself (why can't everyone else?). They were happy to loan me a T-shirt in case Olivia wanted to go for round two and throw my dress in the wash.

I stayed with them for the next few days, observing family life and seeing for the first time what it was like to wake up with children in the morning. I only grew up living with my mother, which was just fine by me. She's an amazing and strong woman,

167

and I had her all to myself. She was everything I needed and more. I never knew or felt like anything was missing from my life, nor do I now. And I'd like to think I was enough for her too. She dated my stepdad Ray from the time I was four until I was fourteen. Nothing about their relationship was normal, yet everything was. My stepfather, who I am extremely close to, has been paralyzed from the waist down since he was run over by a firetruck while riding his motorcycle at the age of twenty-one. So he had his own place, and we would visit him on the weekends where my mother would care and tend to him. It was a big playground of a building that was once an old firehouse.

I'd like to think that I was your average kid getting into mischief when bored. I tested my limits whenever no one was watching. Luckily, I had morals and ethics instilled in me, so I knew my boundaries. Or maybe I always had a guardian angel. This was about the same time I tested authority to the best of my ability. Whenever I got caught doing something selfish and out of line, my mother would have me repent for my sins. Once, she drove me back to a store to return crystal lampshade holders to the store owner and had me apologize. I hated her for it before but now I love her for it.

Chapter 27 - Daddy Daughter Dance

Before I knew it, I had to leave my cousin's and head to my grandmother's wake. It was a long drive flooded with memories. My grandmother must have died of a broken heart. And I was feeling anxious about seeing my father, if he even planned on being there.

The last time my father and I spoke was when he called me one early afternoon, yelling at me after my third round of chemotherapy. He was scolding me and blaming me for him going back to his old ways and drinking again due to me now being sick. This was confusing because he was just drinking at my benefit a little over a month ago. I was hurt, and for some reason, I felt shame. I was ashamed of myself, of him, and of my cancer. He put my illness at a whole new level of hatred. I was silent, probably the quietest I've ever been on the phone. I waited for his mood to shift, to say he was joking or even make a dumb joke like he usually did, but that never came.

He called as I and a few old friends were about to enter an establishment called Paper City, where you pay six dollars and get to drink all the beers you can handle from 6-8 p.m. Then, to top it off, you get to leave with a four pack. Our friend's band was playing there that night and we were all excited to see them perform. A phone call came in as we pulled up. In all the twenty-five years of my life, I can hardly remember when I looked at my phone and saw that it was my father calling. Maybe a few times when I was eighteen?

Naturally, I told them to go ahead, and I'd meet them inside. After all, we only had two hours. I sat there dumbfounded, lost and alone, listening to my father making me feel smaller than I already did. After he hung up, and I can't tell you how the conversation ended, I sat there for what seemed like forever in disbelief. Did that really just happen, or was my brain playing tricks on me again? I was the designated driver since I couldn't drink much while going through chemotherapy. This was the first time I had allowed myself to go out and have a good time since my wig finally came in. I was starting to feel a little better about my appearance in public.

I realized I made a grave mistake. I lost the courage to be out here and see these people. I felt like a hideous monster again, deformed from the inside out. A part of me broke in those few minutes. A part of me I can never get back. It may be one of the saddest things hearing a parent blame their child for their own illness. It's even sadder that this same parent never bothered to call this child again while she was still fighting for her life.

They say you can't pick your family. And even if you could, would you? I know if I had a different father I wouldn't be who I am, and I like who I am. Did it stink not growing up with a kind, nurturing father? Not really. Most people would probably say something different, but they don't have the mother I do.

That was the last time I ever spoke to my father because he did not make it to his own mother's wake or funeral. I later heard through the grapevine that he couldn't go because he was on probation, and he was not allowed to leave the state of New Hampshire. I also heard he violated his probation and had to spend a mandatory six months in jail. I'd like to think he was unable to contact me. But that's just typical me, always giving people the benefit of the doubt.

It was unfortunate that only one of my grandmother's four children was able to attend. The other three were back in New England along with their children. The only people who could make it were my cousin Melissa, her significant other, and their children. Then there was my aunt Yolanda and her daughter Nicole. And rounding out the crowd was my grandmother's sister, her daughter Teresa, and Teresa's daughter.

It was the smallest wake I ever went to. My grandmother looked so skinny. I hardly recognized her at first. Is that what happens when you don't have anyone to cook for anymore? Or is that what it looks like to die of a broken heart? This woman puzzled me as much in her death as she did when she was alive.

We all went out for pizza after the wake, where we talked about how my grandmother and her sister grew up as gypsies in Egypt. I also heard how my grandparents met. Their first date was going to the movies, and my grandmother couldn't go alone with him. She had to have a chaperone. I found it all to be romantically sweet and innocent as it should be. My grandmother had a fascinating childhood. I often wonder if that's where I get my passion to travel from.

Chapter 28 - Better Than a Fortune Cookie

After her funeral service, we all decided to spend the day as a family and explore the Kissimmee and Orlando area. Our first stop was a little theme park that was free to enter on the outskirts of Orlando's big Disney World. We went in and out of shops purchasing ice cream and trinket jewelry. Then someone had an idea about seeing the local psychic a few blocks away.

I vowed never to see a psychic while I was dating someone for fear of what they may say about my love life. But since I was recently single, I was all for it. When we arrived, the psychic, a man, was in his store where you would find various religious artifacts. There were aisles of evil-fighting goodies.

The only problem, this guy didn't speak English. He was from Cuba. Luckily Melissa's significant other was fluent, and he didn't know me, so he was unbiased. I had him sit in with me to interpret what the psychic wanted to tell me. Somehow, we agreed on me going first. He locked up the store, and we headed to a small room outside of the building that looked like it may once have been a shed of some sort. I sat there puzzled, staring at the variety of black and white rocks laid out before me.

He motioned for me to pick up the rocks, shake them in my hands, then drop them back down on the table in front of us. He was a bigger darker-skinned man with telling eyes that pierced into my soul. I felt like these rocks held no significant value because he seemed like he knew everything he needed to know about me with just one glance. I heard psychics can do this but still use props so they don't scare people as much.

I was intrigued by his bag of tricks. The rocks were so smooth and cold to the touch. I probably shook them longer than needed because it was hot in that shed. We went on like that for what seemed like fifteen rounds. Finally, after what seemed like a good five minutes, he began to speak.

For the first order of business, he said, "You came to Florida to find yourself." I nearly lost it. Yes, I was there for a birth, a funeral, and a wedding, but I told myself I was going there to re-find myself. I knew right then and there that whatever he was going to say next would be the whole truth and nothing but the truth, so help me God.

Next, he said, "You just broke up with a guy. That was a good move because he wasn't the right guy for you."

I then asked, "Who's the right guy for me?"

He paused for a moment after the translation and said, "The right guy for you has grays in his hair."

I was dumbfounded because I was only twenty-six. "Wait, you mean to tell me I'm going to fall in love with an albino man?" I replied. "Or am I not going to find the right one until I'm old and gray?"

After a long pause, his response was, "That's not what I am saying."

I took that answer and figured it was better than nothing. Gray hair. Got it. Then he tapped into something else and asked me if I was pregnant. I shifted in my seat wide-eyed and confused, then giggled with satisfaction that I was not pregnant.

173

He asked if I was sure.

I giggled louder, "Yeah, I'm sure." Then I thought to myself, "Does this dress make me look fat? I thought black is supposed to be slimming."

He then repeated what I said and asked, "Did you have an abortion?"

Now I was a little offended for no particular reason and said no with a stern look. He took his time before he went on with the conversation as I gripped the chair underneath me to help stabilize myself better. I told myself to stop fidgeting like a schoolgirl.

"Okay, I got it," he said. "You think you can't get pregnant, but you will. The saints will bless you one time, and due to the circumstances, if you choose to abort, all the saints watching over you will leave your side. And you have a lot watching over you." He paused for a moment, then said, "They also tell me you have made a joking comment in the past that you would go under the knife and have cosmetic surgery. They want me to tell you if you go through with those ideas, they will leave you right then and there on the operating table." He made a clapping reference when he said this in Spanish, where one hand is clapping away from the other, signifying "all done."

Whoa, I thought, *this is intense.* I was so stuck on hearing the last thing he said that I missed the next thing completely. All giggles were gone from that point on. I always joked around that if my big 34 DDD-sized boobs started to sag, I'd pick them back up again. Guess I had better leave it that. I needed all the saints I could get. Maybe that's how I fought cancer and won.

He then said that there was a lesbian girl who was interested in me and for me not to pursue it because it wasn't the right path for me. He also said I better stay away from weed because that would put me on the wrong path. I never had any desire to be with the same sex, and I only mostly smoked when I had cancer to help motivate me to eat, so I figured those were both pretty easy tasks to take care of.

He then said that there was something else he wanted to talk to me about but it was private. So he advised me to call back tomorrow when his wife would be home so she could interpret what he had to tell me. He also suggested that I buy a special spirit-be-gone soap from his shop and bathe with it before I go home because I had some spirits hitchhiking with me from the cemetery. He also told me which saint I should pray to and encouraged me to buy a candle with them on it along with rosary beads.

I was at the point that if this man said I had to walk on all fours, bark like a dog, and quack like a duck for a week, I would've done it. I eagerly bought my goodies, paid him forty dollars for the reading, and skipped out of there like a little girl. I couldn't wait to keep my eyes open for my gray-haired prince. This man made my millennium. The only tragic part is I couldn't reach the psychic when I tried to call days later, and soon after that, he closed his shop.

My cousin Teresa and my aunt Yolanda went next, but he was only with them for a fraction of the time. Nor were their readings as significant. Maybe he used all his spirit charm on me. They told me they wished they went first. I figured my future was crazier than theirs. This is where we all said our goodbyes and separated. I had a lot to think about during my drive to Tampa! My head was spinning. Why did he think I was already pregnant? I was going to be given a chance to have a baby? The doctors told me I was most likely sterile. "Choose to abort due to the circumstances?" What circumstances? I had been careful in the past. I always planned on falling in love, getting married, then having a baby. What would be the reason to think about aborting? Could something be wrong with the baby? Maybe all the chemo and radiation could alter his or her genes? Or maybe, I wouldn't find "the one" until we were both old and gray, and I would develop all sorts of complications. My mind was racing with the possibilities. But I was smiling from ear to ear with the window down, singing along loudly to music as the wind blew through my short hair. If I learned anything that past hour, it was that I was going to have a future. At that point, I would take it any way it came.

Chapter 29 - Shenanigans

I reached Tampa just a little after six, just in time to have dinner with my long-lost friend, Justin. I was the last one to think about joining this potential fiasco of fun, but he convinced me by telling me I would probably have a blast, and I'd fit right in with three guys he used to park ranger with on an island near Boston. I always wanted to be a ranger, so I figured these three guys were just three members of my tribe who I had never met before. I knew about four other people who would be there, but they were all couples and bunking together. Justin's wedding and reception were at a hotel. One of those fun ones, where you can see the wedding going on from the door of your room because it's at the center of the entire complex.

This meant we could see when each other were coming and going and even yell across levels to communicate what shenanigans were in store next. I bunked on a pull-out couch in a room adjacent to Justin's. It was a typical pull-out that made you think you paid enough to stay there, and just maybe it was nice enough that you could upgrade to an actual mattress (turns out, you couldn't). Hey, it was better than staying in my rental that I swore was still an option.

Shortly after arriving, I found out there was going to be a limo that would shuttle us all to the bachelor and bachelorette party. I threw on an outfit that didn't scream "funeral," and I was ready to go. My hair was so short it always cooperated easily enough. After getting ready and meeting everyone in the lobby, I realized

I hadn't seen anyone with gray hair yet. Was I going to find a man in Florida, and if so, would I relocate for him?

I've always considered myself a sun goddess and felt lost in the winter months in the frigid Northeast. However, mountains were my thing, and Florida didn't have a single one. Would I be appealing enough to convert him to being a Massachusetts-lover? Who knows? I decided to try like hell to be open-minded and live for the now as I had been. I always kept my eyes and heart open for that gray-haired man (who was hopefully a bombshell).

We went out to a bar located on the beach, where my friend's girlfriend encouraged me to take lemon drop shots with her throughout the night. The groom managed to be the drunkest of all of us, throwing up on the beach just before we all got back into the limousine. Luckily, our mutual buddy fell asleep on the forty-minute ride back to the hotel. This put a damper on the rest of the night (probably a good thing for our drunker group members), so we all called it an early night. Except, at 3 a.m., Justin decided it would be a good idea to throw a beer bottle off the top deck of the hotel, which then landed on a red car's windshield moments later. The police were called, and the situation was explained to them. They gave him a warning, and he went to bed within the hour.

The next morning was the wedding reception. We all watched as our brains felt like they were banging against our skulls. We were all the opposite from who represented ourselves the night before. We lagged but tried hard to eagerly push forward to see what was in store for the next few days. In the middle of the reception, I realized I flew in last-minute and was unable to bring a gift. Instead of using my car, I and several others who forgot gifts, set out on foot to find them a wedding card or gift.

It was a challenge because we were in a sparsely populated area. First stop, Walgreen's. There, my new friend Jeremy bought Justin a small red toy car, and we smashed the windshield out on the sidewalk so he would always remember the red car he damaged the night before his wedding. We laughed our butts off, but some of us weren't satisfied with just a card and money, so the adventure continued. We stumbled upon Radio Shack (when that was still a thing), where I found a digital picture photo frame that I could slip my digital photo card into. For the next few days, I made it a priority to get the best, craziest pictures possible. I stayed up through all hours of the night, completing my photo album mission. I later found out that this gift was his most favorite wedding gift. And I had a blast doing it.

I took pictures of my roommates sitting on chairs at the bottom of the pool. I took pictures of Jeremy lying on his back being pushed with the luggage cart as he played guitar as loud as he could at 2 a.m. past other hotel rooms. He echoed through the halls, but luckily, his taste in music was soft and sweet to listen to. I took pictures of us taking turns wearing a luchador, Mexican wrestling mask. I even cleverly took pictures through the keyhole of a door as some of us shared a huge "single" sign we found during our walk.

I was happy to give up days and nights working on this gift. The memories were imprinted in my mind forever, and this ended up being the vacation I desperately needed. I will take that week with me for the rest of my life. Because of that week, I grew a great deal on the inside, and I gained a few pounds on the outside as well. I re-found myself that week. It turned out to be everything I hoped for and more.

Chapter 30 - Eenie Meenie

When I returned home, I did some more soul searching and some soulmate searching as well. I was going everywhere and doing everything I could. I thrived on new experiences. I began tagging myself on Facebook with every new place I went. I may have started the whole "selfie" thing, yes, you can pinpoint the demise of society back to me. If I was given a second chance to live, I really wanted to live. Luckily, I had the time to do this without having to go back to work.

I often had anxiety that kept resurfacing about when and if my cancer was going to come back. I'd like to think that's why I kept myself busy. I didn't give myself enough time to sit down and think about everything I went through after I experienced it. I was on to the next thing.

So, after some time, I signed back onto Plenty of Fish. I started to scroll through the male database, and wow, the options were bad. What happened in the past year? It seemed as if the whole dating scene changed, or all the good ones were taken. Regardless, I went to the search engine and plugged in my requirements, tall, dark, and handsome. As I was doing so, I saw there was an option to search for a gray-haired man. I also picked brown eyes. I was never attracted to a man with lighter features. For some reason, it was important to me to find a guy that wouldn't burn every time we went to the beach.

I slowly hovered my finger over the "enter" button, blinked twice, then selected it. But I continued to narrow my search.

For body type, I selected "athletic," "average," and "a few extra pounds." I left the education part blank. I did this because I have met a lot of brilliant people who never went to college but took up carpentry or some other trade and were successful at it. I selected "drinks socially." I was a little bummed there wasn't an option for "drinks responsively."

I was sick of always dating the wrong guy, so I started to pay attention to zodiac signs. I realized Aries, my sign, didn't match well with anyone. I wonder if most single people are Aries as well.

Lastly, I chose ethnicity. I picked Native American and Caucasian. Much to my surprise, I didn't get many results. Maybe I aimed too high when I selected 5'11" or taller. I only stood at 5'3", and I've always been attracted to taller guys. I would like a guy that could pick me up and run with me during a zombie apocalypse.

Only twelve matches. Lucky number twelve. They all fit on one page. This made my life easier. I was going to just do the typical eenie meanie; then I thought about reaching out to the hottest ones first. Hey, don't judge. There were only two men on the page from the age group of twenty-five to thirty-one that I chose who had gray in their hair, and neither of them was attractive in the least bit. I think they exaggerated their age by ten years. Or they had a rough life. Or maybe they just didn't age gracefully. Who knows? I definitely didn't bite to find out.

One guy stood out a little. He was 6'4" and looked Native American. He had "some college" and said his profession was management. The thing I liked the most about him was the ridiculous and goofy profile he put together. He seemed like the laughter I was looking for. It didn't even bother me that he didn't have gray hair. He seemed to have everything else I was looking for.

As I stumbled upon his profile, my phone chimed with a text message from one of my best friends, Amy. She was on her way to pick me up and was letting me know she'd be there in five minutes, which meant twenty minutes in Amy time. I scurried into my bedroom and changed out of my sweats and into a pair of snug jeans and a beaded tank top with a matching cardigan. This was my go-to look back then.

We had planned to go out with the girls to celebrate one of her close friends' birthday. Twenty minutes, right on time, she pulled in front of my house and honked her horn. I shut my laptop, threw on a coat, grabbed a soda, and headed for the door.

It was a typical great night out. We danced, and toward the end of the night, my feet felt like I was walking around on raw meat. But I made it back home safe and sound and made sure I drank enough water so I wouldn't have a hangover in the morning. It was super icy outside, and I even made it back without breaking anything. Luck was on my side.

And speaking of luck, the hottie I was checking out the night before on the dating site must have seen that I checked out his profile because he messaged me. His message seemed to be just as ridiculous as his profile. He didn't take this whole dating thing seriously. There's something I liked about that. He seemed outgoing and sure of who he was. That's always attractive. I couldn't help but look at him and think, *wow, we would make beautiful babies.* The type of babies I probably couldn't have.

I wrote back, being as quirky and cute as I could be. The ball started rolling downhill and fast after those first few days of messaging. We exchanged numbers within the first few hours and decided we would meet that weekend. I wanted to play it cool, so we went to Northampton. Northampton is an earthy, crunchy, freedom, yuppie town. It is popular with feminist movements and proponents of gay rights. It was like having our own Portland, Oregon, right here in Massachusetts.

Many of the homeless people in Northampton probably considered themselves starving artists. On every street corner, someone was playing a romantic melody accepting donations for their long days and over-exuberant personalities. If you went to Northampton and you didn't see the town this way, then you clearly didn't belong there. It was a place for soul searching, to say the least. And lately, that's what I did best.

To my relief, he was all in, and so was I. We first met at the Northampton Brewery. I arrived first and waited at a corner table with a single, lit candle giving me a flickering glow. Luckily, I didn't wait long, but I ordered myself a beer before he showed up. He was soft-spoken and kept fidgeting with his hands under the bottom of his shirt stretching it out in a rhythmic motion. I thought maybe it was a cute nervousness he had, which made me like him more. He also had a little pocket of a belly, but I didn't mind because he was fun.

I learned that his mother was dying at the same time I was given a second chance at life. Somehow, our timelines led us to this very moment. We both talked about how short life was, and we both wanted to thrive on being happy and living for the day. Or so we said.

We spent so much time at the brewery that we almost missed going to The Elevens, a popular music venue, to see a band play. The doors closed in fifteen minutes, and it was at least a fifteen-minute walk. So we threw what money we had in our pockets at the waiter and ran out of there. We took off running down the bike trail at full speed, trying to make it before they closed the doors for good.

Thankfully, we made it in time. He complained he had a bad knee, but it didn't seem to stop him. We went in and danced our way through the crowd, finding each other again as we made our way toward the stage. The rock band played for at least another forty-five minutes, so we danced a bit, and he seemed to enjoy the pheromones excreting from every pore in my body. When they announced last call, I took the chance to steal a random pair of drumsticks. I have been known to do this a lot when I drink beyond my limit. I like to take things, but I would never take anything of significant importance to another person. I would occasionally take a glass or saltshakers from a restaurant. Or if some drunken girl decided to abandon her North Face jacket on the back of a chair for thirty minutes in 10-degree weather, I might take it upon myself to clean up her "mess."

My date reminded me of a panda bear. He was big, goofy, soft, cuddly, and Asian. He surprised me by not fitting into any of the stereotyped boxes I tried to put him in. He seemed genuine, and we just clicked. Plus, I had a feeling like we had met somewhere before and couldn't shake it.

After we left Elevens and Northampton closed down, we started walking along the bike path back to our cars. We talked about what high schools and colleges we went to. We also talked about where we grew up. As we reached my car and said our goodbyes, he gave me the biggest bear hug. We held each other like that for at least a minute. I was cold but warm in his comfort. He reached over and put his hand on my shoulder to say something funny. I knew he was good company because I still felt his touch two minutes after he pulled away. I had just met him, yet he felt so familiar to me.

At this point, I didn't know if he was just going to be another friend or if it could go further than that. I knew I wanted to keep him in my life and didn't want to mess that up with a confusing kiss if I decided we should just be friends.

When I woke up the next morning, old memories washed over me. I called Panda and asked, "Did you used to have a brown satchel you used to wear in college?"

"Yes, I did."

"Whoa. And did you used to always wear pink button-up shirts and white headphones?"

"Yeah, how did you know?"

"Wow. I know where I remember you from. You used to enter building two when I was leaving it like three times a week." In my memory, we would always lock eyes but didn't have a reason to start communicating with each other. I was off and on dating a few long-term boyfriends back then.

Then his memory came back to him. "Oh my God, you're 'The April.'"

I was taken aback a little. I didn't know what that meant, and I waited for him to go on.

He said that a person we both hardly knew at the time turned to him one day as I was walking by and said, "That's April she is so hot, but I guess she's sort of a bitch. You should try to talk to her. She recently became single."

He then told me I had long dark hair back then with blonde highlights, so my hair now threw him off. We were both in shock about this new bit of information. I had to get off the phone with him and think about all of it a little more deeply.

Was this fate? Isn't it funny how people can cross paths again? What did it mean when our eyes connected all those times back then? All I knew was that I was even more excited to see him again.

The next day I was throwing my new roommate a birthday party at this cool establishment called the Hukelau. I figured I should invite Panda and see if he could mesh well with my friends. The Hukelau always brought in famous comedians to do stand-up. It was Hawaiian-themed and had Hawaiian dancing on Fridays. They also had a karaoke night and a lobster night. It was often considered the go-to place for birthdays.

After food and cake, we went to a bar around the block from my house called Sofia's. We figured if we were going to keep drinking, we should be within walking distance of home. I had plenty of space for anyone to spend the night.

In the back of Sofia's, we took over the pool table and the jukebox that played all our favorite tunes. Between all of us, we were never short of quarters or pitchers. As I kept looking over at Panda, I couldn't place it, but something was off due to how I felt about him. I took a bunch of pictures as if they could give me the answers I was looking for. Even after realizing we had met in passing back in college, I still wasn't sure if he was going to get out of the friend zone. I just felt uneasy about the whole thing.

For the record, he slept on the couch that night. And he left for work before I even got up the next day. Those days I would go to bed at 3 a.m. and wake up at noon. Alcohol helped me not have to take any Ativan to fall asleep. I had to make sure I was acquainted with one of those two evils. One felt like I had more control than the other.

Panda sent me a text message while I was sleeping telling me how he had a wonderful time, and he couldn't wait for the opportunity to hang out again. I never responded to his text. I didn't know what to say. It was now a Sunday, and Sunday was Funday, where a bunch of us would go to our friend Josh's house. There we would play board games and indulge in a few beverages followed by a bonfire.

I was starting to get tired from my long weekend when my phone started to ring. Panda called to tell me he was leaving work, and he didn't want to go home. His mother's condition was taking a turn for the worse, and he didn't want to see it. I was already tired, so I agreed he could come over and that I planned on being back home in half an hour anyhow.

I was pretty exhausted by the time I got there. As I pulled into the driveway, he was already waiting for me. At that point, all I wanted to do was lay down and rest. I asked him if he'd like to lie down and talk for a bit, then immediately said, "No funny business."

He laughed and agreed to my terms. As we lay there, he opened up to me some more about his mom and the condition she was in. He asked if I wanted to meet her sometime that week. I said I'd love to. I told him that I may be able to meet her tomorrow. As we were laying there, I looked over and caught a glimpse of something shiny on the back of his head by his neckline. I sat up so fast; I almost fell off the bed. "Wait a minute. You have a gray patch in your hair!" I shouted in excitement.

His response was less intense than mine. "It came out of nowhere, and everyone at work has been teasing me about it lately."

I told him all about my trip to Florida and what the psychic had told me. In that moment, we both felt more destined to be with each other, and almost nothing could change that. From that moment on, we were inseparable, and it drove everyone else around me nuts. I stopped second-guessing how I felt and no longer proceeded with such caution with my heart around him. I allowed myself to fall in love with him with each moment we had together. I loved him even more for continuing to lie innocently next to me every night without trying to make a move. This guy seemed to have been perfect. I felt so lucky to have been re-connected with him, and God was going to fulfill my wish to know what it was like to fall in love.

Chapter 31 - Love Train

At age twenty-one, I thought I loved someone so much that my heart ached when I wasn't with him, and I counted down the minutes until I saw him again. I even got him a job to work with me so I wouldn't have to wait so long to see him. He was more outgoing than me and had a big group of friends and an even bigger group of admirers. He was in a band called "I am Disaster," and I never missed a show. I was always in front screaming all the lyrics to the beautifully written songs.

Dan had a gentleness about him. He spewed positive energy that you just wanted more of. He had beautiful black long wavy hair, big brown eyes, and the most infectious smile that stretched across his face. His soul shined brighter than the sun. And for that, everyone wanted to be around him. I almost had to pencil myself in his calendar on a weekly basis. But any time with him was worth waiting for.

He played the bass guitar and looked like an angel while doing it. There were moments where I swear it looked like he had a halo around his head as he played. It was probably just the lighting playing tricks on me. I loved the way he ate and drank. The way his big lips became wide and thin with each laugh. I even loved the perfectly spaced gaps between his teeth. He would look into my soul when he spoke and blinked while nodding his head in sequence when responding to my questions. He was full of love and life, the perfect combination. I strived to be more like him. But in the process, I started to become more introverted, which was not like me. He started to bring out a side of me I never knew existed. I was so passionate about him in every way that when he didn't live up to his promises, it felt like my heart took a punch.

Toward the end, these punches came more often, and the time in between seeing each other started to increase, largely because he started a new band with my encouragement. This was around the same time I started taking the new Depo-Provera birth control shot, and my hormones were all over the place. I gained fifteen pounds in a few short months and stopped recognizing myself in the mirror. I would just stare at myself, questioning who I had become.

During this time, I bought a house, and I was happy to have him move in with me. I was proud of my accomplishments and having just finished my bachelor's degree in criminal justice. I was on a path to success. I had my full-time job and my part-time job with Dan working as a loss prevention detective for Filene's Basement.

It was cute for a while. The two of us secretly dated behind closed doors, sharing silent kisses when no one was looking. I vowed to stay professional and never go beyond kisses in our shared office. There were times when we were confronted about seeing each other, and luckily, I didn't have Facebook then or even knew what it was. I was still on Myspace.

Shortly after he moved in, Dan started staying out late for band practice so he could learn all the songs and get them right. That was fine with me at first; I wanted a man who felt passionate about something. But the minutes I spent waiting for him turned into hours, and the hours turned into days.

The promises turned into just broken words. If he wasn't coming in as the sun was coming up and I was heading out to work, he would make sure his phone was off so I couldn't chastise him for being out late. When you work in loss prevention, you are often scheduled for late shifts rather than early. I had three jobs; he only had one. I had a house and student loans, and he didn't. I had to have money saved up in case the hot water tank broke. He was saving up for a new bass guitar. So what if we had different priorities? I was a little older by seven months. He had time to catch up.

The day I decided to break my heart was the day I became sick of taking sleeping pills to fall asleep so I could stop worrying if he was okay. This was his famous three-day bender where he didn't step foot in our home once. It was a Saturday-to-Monday, and I called every hospital and jail nearby to make sure he wasn't in trouble.

He called out of work on Sunday, which was time-and-a-half, but he had an important show that weekend, so I covered his shift. I came up with excuses often enough for him until I started sounding like a lying idiot. Realizing this made me second guess who I was and everything I was doing. I looked at myself and asked myself if I was happy. Is this what love was supposed to feel like? I didn't like my answer, and I knew he wasn't going to either.

After a crying fit before I went into work, he came strolling in the driveway hunched over. He looked like only a fraction of the man I once loved. He looked so hopeless it was almost impossible to be mad at him. He didn't have to work that day either. "Please make sure you're home alone when I get out of work at five," I said, shaking my head.

I got home a little earlier than I told him, and he was in the shower. I sat down on the couch, and his phone was on the end table. I waited a few seconds to see if the shower pressure would stop, but it didn't. I decided for the first and last time in my life that I was entitled to see what was on my lover's phone.

I read juicy details of his communication with a woman, "B," who lived in Florida. I wept as I read about how much they loved each other and couldn't wait until their paths met again. I felt like a blind fool and was sick to my stomach. But mostly, I felt unlovable.

By the time he walked out of the bathroom, I was pacing back and forth in the living room. I only read one text message because I didn't want to know if he physically cheated on me. Being cheated on emotionally was way worse, in my opinion. My heart couldn't take any more.

"Who is B?" I snapped, catching him off guard. He stood in the doorway, stuck between a safe place and his worst enemy. At that moment, I realized our roles were reversed, and I was going to be the bad guy for looking at his phone. This pissed me off even more. Instead of him being apologetic for breaking my heart, he was being standoffish and defensive. This is not how I thought this was going to turn out. I thought he was going to ask for my forgiveness and come up with excuses about why he did and said what he did. That is not at all what I got.

Lucky for him, he was already dressed. As our short conversation quickly went from bad to worse, I noticed he started to move toward the exit. This infuriated me even more. I thought, *Okay, so he just wants to leave? Fine. He's hardly been here, anyhow. I am obviously not what he wanted. Something must be wrong with me.*

193

"If you plan on living here, you have a responsibility to be here, and if not, I need to know," I said, my voice shaking.

"If that's the case, I should probably move back home," he said aloofly.

Hearing that, I swiftly took his stupid outdated phone out of his big hands and threw it. I watched in amazement as the woman in me high-fived my other hand. This inspired me to push him out the door. It was the first and last time I ever put my hands on my significant other.

He took a step back and stumbled backward into the mud-room.

As this happened, we locked eyes, and we both heard the pull we once had snap. It was a sad moment, but a moment that needed to happen.

He moved out that week. It was hard to experience that, so I left to go to Lowes to give myself more home improvement ideas to keep me busy. That was the year I decided to put a second-floor addition on the house to keep myself busy. I kept myself busy and stayed like that until I got cancer. I overworked my body for sure.

I didn't anticipate this break-up when purchasing this house. Where would my heart ever be safe again? What is living without loving?

I began to think that my heart was a wasted organ, something inside me that I could never trust again. I decided to take another crack at this whole "love" thing. After all, I had it on good authority from a psychic. And we are supposed to trust and believe them. Right? Just like everything you hear on the internet.

Chapter 32 - Jumping in Blindfolded

This was the first time I could give all my time to someone wholeheartedly without having to work from sunrise to sunset. He had to go to work, of course, but that didn't stop us from seeing each other every night. His mother was in the final stages of ALS, also known as Lou Gehrig's disease. It's a condition that causes the death of neurons that control voluntary muscles. ALS is characterized as having stiff muscles, muscle twitching, and severe weakness due to muscles decreasing in size. This causes difficulty in speaking, swallowing, and breathing.

The cause is unknown in 90 to 95% of cases. And about 5 to 10% inherit it from their parents. About half of these genetic cases are due to one of two specific genes. Unfortunately, there is no cure known for ALS. The disease usually starts around the age of sixty and in inherited cases around the age of fifty. The average survival from diagnosis to death is two to four years. In the United States, the disease affects about two people per 100,000 every year. Most die from respiratory failure.

As the weeks grew on, Panda went home less and less. It was excruciating for him to see his mother in that condition. Both his father and his brother lived there. Panda's brother Bryan worked long hours. He also kept himself busy so he wouldn't have to see his mother in that state for long periods of time. Panda's father has also battled cancer three times in his past. He was retired and able to stay home and take care of her as she had done for him. There was a hired nurse who popped in from time to time.

I learned my house had become a haven for him. We felt comfortable with each other in such a short amount of time. It felt like all the stars were aligned, and I was exactly where I was supposed to be. My roommate, who just moved out, asked me for a ride to run a few errands. I told him I could because I wanted to make sure we remained friends. I also told Panda the night before I would meet his mother. Unfortunately, my new roommate's errands ran long, and I missed the window to see Panda's mother. I felt awful about it. We were both looking forward to it, and I couldn't apologize enough.

I know he was disappointed, and it was the first time I ever disappointed him, so it hung over me like a cloud. I was excited to see this cute little Filipino woman. I wanted to pick her brain and see what type of man her son was.

After that day, her health deteriorated horribly. She closed her eyes and stopped talking altogether. It was hard to live with myself knowing I had a window of an opportunity to meet the mother of someone I had fallen completely in love with. It would have been an important and special moment, and I blew it. My heart ached for him. I felt like there was nothing I could say or do to make it right. I have never seen such a large man crumble. I held him for hours. I remember how wet my lap was. My clothes were stuck to me from all his tears, and his head weighed so much. I just kept stroking his hair, telling him it would be okay. He cried so hard he shook, and I remember trying to hold him still.

That moment I knew how much I loved this man. I would do anything to take away his pain and make him whole again. I said a prayer to his deceased mother and told her I would watch out for her son. I would love him and protect him as long as he'd let me.

A few days later, her funeral took place. I arrived late; I went to the wrong cemetery. Ware happens to have the most cemeteries in all of Massachusetts. This is because they flooded four towns north of Ware to make the Quabbin Reservoir. This is the largest inland body of water built between 1930 and 1939 to become Boston's water supply. The towns they disincorporated were Enfield, Dana, Greenwich, and Prescott.

When I mentioned to my mother that I was going to attend her funeral she said, "It must be at the Quabbin Park Cemetery."

I assumed she was right because I did not want to bug Panda. I knew he had enough on his plate. So I cemetery-hopped until I found the right one. As I pulled up, I saw his brother hug somebody in the parking lot. He screamed uncontrollably into that person's neck. I thought it was Panda at first until I saw this person was much smaller in stature. My heart broke a little. I took a deep breath as I entered a crowd of people grieving. The only person I knew there was Panda. I was so fixated on him. I studied him from afar. He looked great, dressed impeccably.

As I looked on, I was amazed because he looked so well put-together inside and out. I think he was working on trying to keep it together for everyone else. It gave me a little insight into how he must have felt for me because he allowed himself to break down and completely lose it in front of me. A person he should have felt safe to be vulnerable with.

As I glanced around, I noticed I saw someone I knew. Her name was Marsha, and we went to school together. She was friends with his mother through her best friend, who was also Filipino.

I find myself being too intuitive for funerals. I typically try to avoid them. All it takes is one person in my peripheral vision, and I completely lose it. I looked around while his brother gave a speech, and I saw only one person sob into what looked like their mother's arms. She had blonde hair and wore capris and high heels in winter weather. I thought that was odd. I later found out it was Panda's ex (that explained her trying to dress up). I must have changed my outfit five times before I decided on a pair of slacks and a black blouse. I was nervous to meet so many important people in his life under such harsh circumstances. I couldn't be my happy goofy loud self because this was not a joyous time. I felt a little out of place, but Panda did a good job making me feel like I belonged. So when his father brought back a couple of pitchers of booze after the services, I indulged in a glass to calm my nerves.

At the end of that day, Panda came back to my house for comfort. His brother went to his girlfriend's house, and his father went home to the bottle. Life stayed like that for a while. Panda nearly moved in. His car trunk was his wardrobe.

Two weeks after his mother passed, I made the adult decision to lay down with him. I had grown to love the man. We didn't complete the deed. We were both too excited and nervous.

Panda was given a leave of absence from work for four weeks after his mother perished. He had two weeks left, and he decided he wanted to buy a 350 Z, his childhood dream car. I told him I didn't think it was ideal, but I went with him anyway to go "look at it." The car dealership gave him an offer he couldn't refuse. They locked him in at a 3.8% APR rate after they ran it through fifteen different financial brokers, which we later found out ruined his credit. To his defense, I understood he needed something positive, something different and exciting in his life. I knew this before he even went to see the car.

He looked down at me with puppy dog eyes and said, "If I buy this car, we are going to take off to Canada." He actually asked me for permission. I couldn't say no because I knew his mind was already made up. I agreed because I knew he needed support. The kind of support his mother would have given if she was here.

And to be honest, I was a little excited to have a rendezvous with him away from my roommates. Plus, it had been a long time since I had been to Canada. I started to get butterflies thinking about it.

I was excited about Canada but not about this little death trap of a car he was dead set on buying. Before he signed the paperwork, I commented, "Where are you going to put the car seat?"

"By the time I'm ready to have a child, the car will be paid off, and I'll buy a second car," he said with a smile.

Before I decided to run off to another country with him, he had to at least meet my mother. My mother is a good judge of character. So, back to Ware we went. At this point, my mother had been living with my stepdad for eleven years. They were more like roommates. They lived separate lives under the same roof. He worked roofing all day, and she stayed home like the nice little housewife she could be and cleaned, cooked, and sold bottles on eBay to make money and pass the time. He would come home from work, tend to the yard, eat, and then go upstairs to his own bedroom and play Call of Duty, have a beer, smoke a doobie, tell her goodnight, and do it all over again the next day. They lived like this for too many years.

This was not the type of relationship she wanted for me. As a parent, you always want more for your child than what you had for yourself. I know she wanted more from hers. I think she was afraid to be more alone than she already was. At least someone came home to her at the end of the day.

When I moved out of my mother's house at age seventeen, I don't think she was ready to let me go yet. I created a hole in the pit of her being. One she tried to fill with him. One no lover could fill because it was a different type of love, an unconditional one that no words in any language can properly put into perspective. My mother was a saint for putting up with me in my hormonal years and putting up with him in his selfish ones. I don't think he meant to be selfish. He had to learn how to not rely on anyone in his early years.

I think toward the end, he made her feel like a rubber tree in the dark corner of the room. The kind that looked beautiful yet did not need to be watered.

Panda and I went to check on his father's wellbeing. I walked in not expecting to see what I saw. We were in and out quickly. The smell smacked me in the nose first. His father was not in his best shape. He was on a bender from the day before, and by the looks of him only in his boxers, you could tell he was not ready for company.

Oh, my sweet Panda, I thought. This is how you're living?

At one point, I noticed the blown-up picture I gave him of his mother playing in the ocean in the Philippines. She looked so peaceful.

I later found out that was the last trip she took there. She was born and raised there until she was thirty. Then she ventured to L.A., where she met his father eight years later. She was a forty-year-old virgin by the time she married him. I loved that about her. You could tell by the photo she was a sweet but feisty woman.

The house was on the busiest street in town. His mother never bothered to get her license. You could also tell her children were her world.

After saying a quick goodbye to Panda's dad, we trekked to my mom's house about a dozen minutes away.

My mom opened the door with a big hello and generous hugs. I told him she heard a lot about him. But I only gave her a glimpse of him and a short background about us. I don't bring everyone home to meet her. The guys I considered dating long-term, I did. I did tell her I was unsure about him, something was holding me back.

She took her time studying him throughout the visit. She asked appropriate questions, trying to find his motive for wanting to be in my life and where he saw it going. His answers were sweet and direct. She liked him, and since she liked him, I liked him more. It was like I got her approval to get lost into him. After helping us stuff our faces, we left to go get lost in each other.

Chapter 33 - They Have Jungles in Canada?

The next day, we filled up his 350Z and headed to Canada. We snapped a bunch of happy pictures on our way there as I Googled possible hotels to stay in. I found one that fit our budget. It was marked #63 in Montreal, and it seemed quirky and resembled more of an inexpensive boutique of wood and shenanigans. I was all for it. One thing that bothered me about Panda was he never "treated" me to anything. He was always tight with his money and was never too generous. We were polar opposites in that regard because I have been and always will be a giving person. If I offered to pay for the whole trip, I knew he would let me, even if I was on a fixed income.

I forgot how cold Canada was. We initially parked out front until we checked in. The snowbanks made it difficult to park his tiny 350Z. The hotel was made of white brick and had pointless black cast-iron fences that never met with a gate to enter. Above our heads was a red makeshift sign with Aubrey Hepburn's face smoking her famous cigarette to the left, blowing out smoke that said "Celebrities," the name of our hotel. At our feet was a red carpet laid out in front of us, leading to the door. I couldn't help but laugh out loud. Each of the twenty-six rooms was decorated with celebrities on the walls, and all were different shapes and sizes. It was eclectic and much funkier than the Holiday Inn!

There was a tall counter with a young long haired blonde man with a big nose who checked us in but only spoke in French, but he was trying his hardest to communicate with us and tell us what he recommended. We knew we were going to be there for two days, so we chose a different room for each night to switch it up a bit. Panda took French in high school and was eager to try to teach me some on the way. I got the basics down like "hello," "goodbye," and "thank you." I never want to come across impolite. I think it's sexy when a guy you're dating can speak multiple languages. I always wished I spoke at least one other language. I dabbled in Spanish and Chinese for a few years in high school, but nothing stuck for too long.

It was a bit of a turn-on. I liked the idea of thinking he was tall, dark, handsome, and smart. After the foreign exchange, we headed upstairs to the jungle room we picked out. On the way up, the walls were all red and had 3D blocks sticking out of them. We packed light, so the twenty or so stairs we had to climb weren't too bad. We opened the door and saw that the walls were a colorful royal blue glaze. The same glaze was high above our heads and formed an arch. It was like they hired a middle schooler to paint the place. They even attempted to make a mural on the wall, adding a splash of yellow. And the only light the room seemed to have were tiny spotlights aiming at different areas of the "art" in the room.

I took off my shoes and went exploring. The floors were dark wood, making the room seem smaller than it was. There was a rope hanging to my left that seemed to serve no purpose, but I remember thinking I wanted to swing from it like Tarzan. The bedsheets caught my eye next. The bedspread was zebra print with matching curtains, and there was a white padded bench to kneel on before getting into bed. The bed frame was also made from the same dark wood sealed in a glaze. Then my eyes darted to a large wooden carved statue to the right of the bed. It resembled a fake tree. Behind the curvy white couch next to the bed were two by four pieces of curved dark wood making a pattern that resembled the iron throne from Game of Thrones. I glanced back at Panda and gave him a look like, how unreal is this place? There was a small silver TV hanging to the right that was way too small and outdated for that room. We later concluded that this was the last room they made, and they built it from the scraps of the other rooms. It made me love it that much more!

I then noticed a door leading to outside. I fiddled with the locks and finally made my way out. It was a little hard to open the door at first with the four inches of snow left on the ground, but it was worth it because we had our own private balcony. I felt like a little girl all over again. I turned around and shut the door after he took a peek and noticed the cute little white fake fireplace in the corner next to the bathroom.

The bathroom was even weirder than the room. You had to walk down into the small tub they created. It had a basic toilet to the right and a sink to the left, too mundane for the rest of the intricate room. We threw our backpacks on the bed, snapped a few pictures, then set out to move the car and explore Montreal.

We were within walking distance of the University of Quebec-Montreal and a strip that had the city's best entertainment, which helped because we had no idea what the parking situation would be. The only problem with this was the cold, and I only had my thin North Face jacket.

Needless to say, we didn't do too much walking. All the street names were named after saints, so they all started to sound the same after a while.

We happened to be on the "porn-ish" strip of Montreal, where ladies were shaking their hush puppies in one place and then selling sex toys in the next. Of course, we went into one of the shops. We had our laughs, and yes, we bought some stuff and then headed back. We didn't want to do anything else but be together, and I was fine with that. We stopped into a package store and picked up a bottle of Jack Daniel's new honey whiskey and proceeded to do shots back at the room. For the record, I am not a shot person, but I recently sampled this drink while going into a liquor store and thought I was in love. He stuck to the Guinness he picked up.

I've always loved this motto: "If a key opens lots of locks, then it's a master key, but if a lock is opened by lots of keys, then it's a shitty lock." It had been so long since I had sex that even the number three was starting to turn me on. I don't remember how it started. I probably said something stupid like, "I want you to dinglehopper me!" I then made love to him like it was my last night on Earth. He was my "Make a Wish." Remember I told God He could not take me yet because I hadn't truly fallen in love yet? Was this it? We finished off the night making naked snow angels on our private balcony while I thanked mine.

Chapter 34 - Horseshoes and Hand Grenades

When I was little, I used to pick a bunch of what looked like bay leaves off a bush at the stoop of my house. I would then walk two houses down to the end of the street, where I would drop a petal about every other sidewalk block. I would hope that my prince charming would find the path, find me, and sweep me off of my feet. He never came.

Fast forward to today, I am glad he never came because I wasn't ready growing up and maturing, I have seen men absolutely destroy women. Breaking them down into something they were never destined to be. I never fully let a man get too close to me in the hopes of avoiding being in that lifeless state. I don't think I would ever be ready for that hurt. To be so vulnerable, to be so exposed, to be so open. I could never give someone that much power over me.

I would love to say Panda changed all this for me. That he enabled me to open up and give myself wholeheartedly like I had always wanted. He was my "Make a Wish," after all, wasn't he?

But this isn't a love story. This is a story about tragedy and heartache...but what doesn't kill you makes you stronger, I suppose. Panda turned out to be a mean and angry person who didn't hesitate to take the frustrations of his life's pains on me. They say opposites attract. They couldn't be more right. He used me like a punching bag with hateful words. He would say the most rotten things to me that anyone has ever said. He would say anything to try to get a rise out of me and tear me down. I cried so much in the beginning. I could fill a pool with the tears I shed because of him. This was like some sick joke bringing me back from the dead, only to torture me.

I know, why didn't I just leave him, right? I didn't leave him because the first time we had sex in Canada, he got me pregnant. I felt stuck and alone and fat, and those were all the things he reminded me that I was. In the beginning, I never fought back. I just cried my heart out on the cold bathroom floor, feeling like I was the size of a whale, while he still was attacking me with insults and evil words on the other side. I desperately hoped he would realize how bad his words were hurting me and would comfort me and kiss the tears from my face. But he never did. He never apologized after he worked so hard to knock me down.

Instead, he would start joking about something almost immediately after he broke me down to nothing. It was like he could flip a switch in a game that only he was playing. At one point, I thought I was going to have to answer the door to the police doing a wellness check because the neighbors must have heard him screaming at me. His abusive actions made no sense. After trying to search for answers, I came up with two things. One, he had to be bipolar, or two, this kind of behavior was modeled in his household while growing up.

After months of trying to pinpoint what triggered him, I learned to stop crying when he attacked me. I learned to be quiet as I set up our future son's crib as he watched from afar, hands behind his head laying in our bed, calling me fat. He threw his own insecurities onto me as I realized later since he gained sixty pounds while I was pregnant.

I also found that not responding to him would also make him irate. He would say the worst possible things that he stored in a secret safe, and he would use them as a weapon to cut me deeply. His grand finale of abuse and insults usually involved something about my father abandoning me, which to him meant I was unworthy of love. So I switched up my tactics.

I began to stand my ground and refused to continue to be a victim. I fought back. I gave him a piece of his own medicine. I no longer cried every time. I stopped feeling sad and sorry for myself, I began to get angry with him and the situation I was in.

All I wanted was my mother when he came at me. I wanted to feel safe again. I knew being around her, he wouldn't attack me as much, so I asked her to come over every day. Whenever she couldn't, I would cry because I was unsure how my day would turn out. I was living my life in fear for me and my son. I felt like I was drowning and couldn't tell which way was up for air.

All my friends stopped coming around right when I needed them the most. They were sick of hearing my horror stories about Panda. They no longer recognized this weak and helpless person I had become. They stopped calling me back and then got together and told me if I wanted to be their friend, I had to break up with him because they were sick of hearing it. I had to tell someone I needed to release the anguish and hurt I was feeling. When you have a fight with someone you need to tell someone. My mother was the last person in my life to stick by my side, but Panda worked hard to separate us. He would go so far as to tell her things I said about her and vice versa. Everything he said was fabricated, and my mother didn't believe him.

I was so unrecognizable I bet I could not have picked myself out of a police lineup. I looked like a woman who had been eaten from the inside out. He emptied me of any happiness and joy. Sometimes the quiet in your head can be incredibly loud. He put himself above me just to love me. Whenever he tried to be nice, he spoke in the third person. It was awful. And with Panda, I did everything, even at nine months pregnant.

I tried encouraging him to go to anger management. I even tried threatening he would never have us as a family if he didn't try to control his temper. I encouraged him to go for walks, to count down from ten. To even leave and come back. To do whatever he needed to do to try to keep us as a family together. He failed at all of them. He never followed through. Nothing stuck. If it wasn't for my son, I would have encouraged death to try to take me again. I could no longer see the light and everyone who knew me saw the light vanish from my eyes. It got so bad I deleted all of my social media accounts and went into hiding. I felt ashamed that I had praised someone so much publicly, only to be mocked by him any chance he got.

I had one person who I was eager to invite as part of my wedding party, who replied with nothing more than, "Good luck with that." I needed people to tell me I was going to be okay, to help build me back up and make me strong again. Instead, everyone I loved showed me I was unworthy of love. The very thing Panda had taunted me with.

After breaking up with someone, you always wonder what they tell others about the reason for the split. When I was younger, I cared deeply about how people saw me. I struggled with it to the point of paranoia. I just wanted everyone to love me. Even though that seems like a horrible characteristic, it also drove me to do my best in everything I set out to do. I gave everything I had with passion and love. It drove me insane that after

I gave my all, some people were okay to write me out of their lives. Wasn't I still worth it after all the effort I gave? Worthlessness is one of the worst feelings.

The loneliness in me started to interrogate me. My biggest fear used to be dying alone. But after going through everything with Panda, I realized that was now a goal.

Eventually, Panda got tired of using the same lines over and over again. So he tried a different method. He said if I left him, he was going to run away with my son to the Philippines, where his family was, and I would never see him again. And I wouldn't be safe there trying to search for him because I was a petite blonde with blue eyes, and they would rape me, beat me, and if I was lucky, kill me.

He used this on me far more than I'd like to admit, and I believed him. I knew he was capable of this because he grew tired of yelling, and now, he started breaking things when he got angry. Let's just say it got so bad that when he was starting to "argue" with me over something, I immediately locked myself in a room with my child to protect us. I would have 911 on my phone with a push of a button. But I was scared to do that too because one of his best friends just joined the local police department.

The most helpless I ever felt with him was running to a room I knew would lock, grabbing my son on the way, but forgetting my phone. I knew time would not be on my side because chances were my son would be hungry before Panda was done being angry.

I had no idea what set Panda off, and that was the scariest part. I never knew why or when the bullets would be flying my way.

One day, I finally understood I needed to do something when I had nowhere to run because he learned my new escape route and blocked the bedroom door. I had no choice but to go downstairs to my neighbor, who also happened to be my aunt, that I rented the first floor of my house to after we moved upstairs to the new addition and no longer had any roommates. I couldn't leave because I had no shoes on, and all I knew was I needed to get far away from this man as fast as I could. I heard him yelling after me, asking me where I was taking his son and how I had no right to leave.

I counted my blessings that they finally came home, and my cousin Corey was home too. I needed a man like Corey to protect me. I never even knocked on their door; I ran in and locked the door behind me. I then made sure the big sliding window was also locked because otherwise, he could easily climb through. He called his bodybuilder brother to come over so they could kick my cousin Corey's ass together. He only weighed about 160 lbs.

They lured him out and intimidated him into a fight where he stood his ground to protect me. I sat in her rocking chair, squeezing my son to my chest as I refused to answer any of their questions. I kept saying to myself, "You're safe, you're safe." I rocked and rocked with tears streaming down my face, clutching my child as a big, 260 lb. man was trying to make his way through the door, threatening to call the cops because I was keeping him from his child. I realized while rocking my son that I was, in fact, not safe. I was only safe in that moment because my aunt got home in time.

Chapter 35 - Backpedaling

I could not go on any longer like this. I needed to find a way out. So I decided to sell my house and move into my mother's house "as a family". I left the house I worked so hard for so many years to make sure I would never be alone with a man like this again. I felt like a dummy, and he was the ventriloquist. I thought maybe in the presence of my mother, this big man, the father of my child, would stop being so mean to me. I would be safe with my mother, right? My stepfather, who ran me out of the house once before, was not enthused about the idea of me, Panda, and my dog Lady moving in. But he enjoyed having my son Maddox in the house. Maddox had a way of melting his heart.

Now, my mother, son, dog, and I were living with two hot-headed men. On the very first day, my stepdad complained about how lazy Panda was because he wouldn't put in as much effort as my stepdad while moving our things in. "Lazy" was the title given to Panda for many months until he finally had enough. He had to take his frustration out on someone. So, eventually, everything became the dog's fault. He yelled at her the most over just about anything. She is a great dog, but with Panda now one of her owners, she started doing all the wrong things that went against how I had raised her. He started giving her scraps of food from his hand while we were eating. This gave her the idea that she was an equal. Now, every time we sat down to enjoy a meal, Lady would be begging and driving us all nuts.

My stepdad started taking his food into a different room than us and avoided any type of interaction except using his headset that projected voices from playing Call of Duty.

This was a world he was in control of. He was able to let off steam, blow people up, and swear as much as he wished. He gave himself his own hideaway in the house. It was the smallest room, but it was all his. We learned not to enter it and to tiptoe by whenever we had to go into the living room from the kitchen.

Panda also made his own hiding area in the house. He chose the basement. His little room consisted of a TV, old couch, Xbox, and a bong. If he would come home and didn't want to engage with anyone, he would kiss Maddox on the head and head straight down to the basement, where I wouldn't see him until dinner time. I almost treasured these days the most.

I had the master bedroom, the same one I briefly had when I was seventeen. Before I moved into the room, my stepfather had to move out of it. He had been living in it separately from my mother for six years. Their romance came to a screeching halt when he decided she snored too loud.

After learning this, she tried to correct it. She purchased snore strips and even went to see multiple doctors, but they told her since she had a deviated septum, she would continue to snore unless they broke her nose again.

One day, my mother was staring at my stepfather, wondering if she should break her nose for the fourth time to see if it would solve their problems. But while gazing at him, admiring his beautiful facial structure, he snapped his head toward her and asked what she was staring at.

She thought this was a good indication that maybe she should just leave her nose right where it was. My mother used to tell me, "April, all men are assholes. It's your choice what type of asshole you want to live and deal with." Shortly after we moved in, my stepdad moved out.

And soon, Panda started to work his charm on my mother every night while I slept. He would push himself to stay up late to share cigarettes with her night after night. He worked his way under her skin like he did with me. Then the games began. He started his manipulation. She was his last target, the last person I cared about. He would tell her I was acting irrationally, over-reacting, and emotionally imbalanced. I started to notice my mother reacting differently to things I would say. She never knew eighty percent of the things he would say or do. I was embarrassed to have been stuck with such a vile person.

I wanted my son to grow up with both parents and have what I never had. But under my mother's roof, I grew silent and weaker. I didn't even know that was possible. During this time, I made a bond with my son that will last forever. I even spoke for him when he lacked the words. Everyone was amazed that I knew what he wanted before he tried to express it. He was my reason for living. He was my new Make a Wish. I told God He couldn't take me yet because I hadn't found true love. So he gave it to me in the way I needed it the most, with a son. I realized this after I knew I was not in love with Panda anymore. I realized the purpose of everything, even though it wasn't what I had envisioned for my future. Then I remembered what the psychic said, and the understanding hit me like a bright warm light. This was my destiny.

I realized my soul's purpose was to raise this little boy and to love his life as much as I loved him. This realization made Panda powerless over me. I started to fight back. I wanted my life back, and I was ready to do whatever it took. First, I needed my mother to see clearly again. I needed someone in my corner. So I started to record him whenever he came after me. I needed her to know I wasn't overreacting, I wasn't instigating, and I wasn't the one sabotaging my family.

Panda caught on after a while and started saying things that made him sound innocent. I realized that if he could change himself like that, then he was crazier than I thought. This man was a cancer of a different kind, trying to finish the job that had started before I went into treatment. And I knew how to fight cancer, and I decided I would fight like hell to rid myself of this deadly Panda-carcinoma.

Chapter 36 - A Lonely Road and Not Such a Long Way Down

Something woke me up around 6:30 a.m. and I couldn't go back to sleep, so I figured I might as well get Maddox's bottle ready and warmed up. As I started walking downstairs, I noticed an odd, unfamiliar smell. I started pacing in search of where it was coming from. I couldn't figure it out, and something inside me told me to wake up everyone in the house. I woke Panda up, and he reluctantly followed after a few minutes. I had always had a hard time smelling or relating smells, but he was quick about it. He followed the scent to the basement, and then we started to hear an alarm go off. I initially thought it was the UV system we recently installed so the baby would have purified water.

I left him to investigate as I ran up two flights of stairs and grabbed towels to shove under Maddox's door since the scent grew stronger. Then I woke up my mom as I nearly tripped over my ninety-pound dog, who was sneezing and pacing the hallway. I woke my mother up and ran down the stairs again. My mother fought her way past Panda as she attempted to search the basement for the smell. She decided the smell was so bad that it would be easier to make it to the UV system from the basement door. She figured the smell would draft out the door, clearing the house a bit more. She then yelled at me to get Maddox out of the house as she dialed 911.

I raced up the stairs, grabbing his jacket. I still had his bottle upstairs, so I shoved it into his mouth after I got his jacket on him. My trusty dog Lady was at my heels, and we left the house. Meanwhile, downstairs when my mother opened the basement door, she fed the newly discovered fire with oxygen. Just like that, the basement went up in flames.

I couldn't find the keys to my car on my way out. So I got Maddox situated in my mother's car, which was furthest from the house. Fortunately, she had her keys since she needed them to open the cellar door. I sat in the car, staring at the house, more numb than I've ever felt before. My world was literally crashing down around me. How did it come to this? Every noise was drowned out, and all I could hear was a loud ringing in my ears. My mother broke the silence as she screamed, "The birds!" Just then, a police officer and my mother attempted to go back into the house to get to the birds' room. Her efforts were not fruitful. The smoke was too thick for my mother and the officer to get to the room. My mother had three parrots that helped fill the void in her empty house, and now they were gone too. Finally, tears started streaming down my face.

The flames grew larger and stronger before the local fire department arrived. It was the longest eighteen minutes of my life. Looking at the shape of the smoke reaching the sky, it was clear that everything we once had was gone. My mother called the fire department (where she happened to work) one more time before they reached our street, screaming in sheer panic. "Where are you? I am losing my house." She was shaking and on the verge of throwing up in the driver's seat next to me.

I stared straight ahead in total disbelief. It was like my body hit the pause button, and the play button was ripped off and thrown out the window. I couldn't believe it. The day before, we had gone shopping for Thanksgiving. We bought three hundred dollars' worth of groceries. Where would our family go now?

The fire trucks finally came roaring in, surely waking all the neighbors who were still nestled into their beds, ripping them away from their dreams.

As smoke started to escape from every crack in the house, we listened as the firefighters broke all the windows in the basement. We then watched as they opened all the windows throughout the house. Because they didn't smash all the windows, I thought that had to be a good sign as I clung to what little hope I had left. My mother went by ambulance to the local hospital to be checked for smoke inhalation since only she went back into the house.

Next, the vultures came in. Every fire restoration company near and far came to push their business on us, promising us the world one business card at a time. It was quite sickening. I didn't have the stomach to deal with them, so I went to greet the Red Cross van that showed up. They gave Maddox a teddy bear that he still cherishes to this day. They also gave us a little bag for hygiene like toothpaste and brushes, and a Visa gift card with fifty dollars on it so we could get some of the basics like socks and underwear. That small but powerful gesture went a long way.

After about an hour and forty-five minutes of tackling the flames, re-shutting the windows, and trying to investigate how the fire started, their work was finished. They re-extracted the pool of water they made outside of the house, handed me my car keys, picked up their equipment, and left.

There was nobody in our family that was able to re-home three adults, a two year old, and a ninety-pound dog. So we needed to go to a hotel big enough to accommodate us and a dog. Ware had no hotels, so that meant my mother would be out of work because she was on call and needed to stay in town. We picked the fire restoration company the same way we picked our hotel, from a recommendation.

We were not allowed to go back into the house and get anything due to the smoke damage. So we made our way to a Wal-Mart to grab a few essentials and some pet food. Our next stop was a hotel in West Brookfield, close to our house. They placed the four of us in a suite, which only consisted of a mini-fridge, two stove burners, and two beds. My mother decided to get her own room. Panda, me, and Maddox were alone, together again, in a nearly empty echo-y room with no toys and a very confused dog.

I took one look at my son and knew I needed to be strong for him. So I made a safety tent out of pillows and extra sheets I found in an open closet that had no doors. After he grew tired of that, we bowled with the tissue paper. The next morning, we woke up to a blizzard.

Even though I had four-wheel drive, I knew it would be too risky going up and down a large hill, which was our only way out of the hotel. So we stayed put and tried to be grateful that we were all still alive.

At one point, I ran out to the car to see if I could find any loose toys in my jeep for Maddox to play with. Running back up the stairs, I found a very puzzled and disoriented bird on the ground. I picked it up carefully and ran it to my mother's room in the next building over. Over the next few days, she nursed it back to health. We believed this could have been an omen from God letting her know her birds were alright, and that it was time to stop mourning the loss of them.

After our three days were up at this hotel, we were off to the next one. This one was in Chicopee. A city I have never lived in before. It was about thirty minutes away from our house but fifteen minutes away from where I grew up with friends and family.

At this hotel, the four of us and my dog had to share a two-bedroom space separated by a small kitchen. My mother and Panda went to work every day as I stayed "home" with my son. This hotel came with a pool and free happy hour served Monday through Wednesday, along with a free meal.

I believe people are either running from something or running to something. I didn't want any more beef from anyone; I just wanted to be a vegetarian. At this point, I started to drink. And I don't mean fall-down drunk, but a few drinks at the end of the night to numb my pain and brokenness. I was just so tired of feeling. I experience the world's sadness as my own, and it was and is exhausting. In a world full of disaster, disorder, and rejection it was hard for me to find the truths.

Then the day came where Panda and I finally had to part ways. I am a woman of my word. I always have been, and I always will be. When I break up with someone, there is no going back. I already thought about the pros and cons, and once the cons outweighed the pros by a large margin, it was time to throw in the towel. I was living miserably and only so my son could grow up in the same household with both of his parents. But that meant he had to grow up seeing his mother cry and sad all the time. And with a father who was constantly yelling and arguing. That living arrangement is less ideal than a broken family.

We were living in a four-hundred square foot area in a hotel stepping on each other's toes and told we may be there for over a year. The complaints came in more frequently, especially two hotel rooms over, neighbors calling the front desk to say there was a domestic dispute going on. My mother's insurance company was paying for us to be there. What would happen if they kicked us out? We had nowhere else to go.

It was important for me to make sure my son never thought he was a mistake just because we didn't plan him. But when his father actively told me he wished he never met me in front of Maddox, it was the final straw.

The day we ended it was actually preceded by a good couple of days between the two of us. I thought I had been good enough to possibly leave for a couple of hours that night, which I never did. It was Super Bowl Sunday, and Panda said he didn't want to do anything but stay at the hotel and watch it there. That morning, I told him I was invited to join a friend to watch the game at her brother's new mansion. Panda had no issues with me leaving. Either because we just had sex, or maybe because he was feeling generous.

As the day grew on, he grew snippier and snippier. Then he went into a full-on rage. After he went on like this for about an hour, our hotel phone rang. There was a noise complaint. This was the third one since we lived here. I thought maybe my presence was making him worse, so I asked him if he could leave for a couple of hours and then come back. After fighting some more, he agreed and slammed the door on his way out, saying he was going to his friend's house to watch the game and would be back late. At this point, I was fine to see him go. He could have been gone for a week, and I would be perfectly fine with that. Except, he didn't like my response.

He wanted me to get angry and fight back, probably thinking I would be upset that he ruined my plans with my only friend left. But my main concern was that we didn't get kicked out of the hotel that our insurance was kind enough to cover. It was the best hotel for miles, and they even allowed dogs. What would we tell our insurance company? How incompetent would we look? Would they even cover another hotel? Would we have to come up with the money before we got approved? Would I have to ask someone to watch my dog for the remaining months? Could my dog survive that? Who could even do that? Would I have to get rid of her?

Panda kept screaming and shouting, so I took our son and went downstairs into the lobby to play on the public computers putting "Gummy Bears" on repeat, hoping to distract him. This lasted for about ten minutes until I heard a commotion behind us. Through the see-through fireplace, I saw Panda glaring at me about sixty feet away. He had one hand out toward the clerk, waiting for her to put several new room cards into his hand. I knew he was up to no good. Was he going to ask her to reset the locks and lock us out of the room?

As this was going through my head, he knocked me out of my trance by screaming, "What are you looking at?"

Now I was mortified and embarrassed. He had no regard for anyone around him, evident by the scene he was creating. My soul slouched into my gut. Who was this man I once loved so much? How did we become this? I got up quickly and headed into the elevator with my son in my hands. I pressed the shut door button and prayed he wouldn't make it inside where I would have nowhere to go. As the elevator door was shutting, he yelled, "Where are you going with my son?"

It was clear I was going upstairs to our room, praying the key I had in my back pocket was still active. Luckily it was. I got inside and started pacing. What was his next move? What should my next move be?

Then a loud voice popped into my head, *You were not given a second chance at life to live it like this.* It was as if God himself whispered those words to me.

Then boom, he came barreling through the door and began berating me. But finally, I had something to say back. "I was not given a second chance at life to live it like this."

"Fine," Panda yelled back. "Then I am leaving for good. You will finally get what you've been wanting." He picked my son off the couch to give him a huge hug goodbye. But like any young kid who has witnessed his father throwing a tantrum for four hours, he tried to squirm away.

This infuriated Panda more than anything, so he roughly tossed Maddox onto the couch and said, "Fine. You are going to grow up without a father just like your mother did. There. Now history will repeat itself."

As I rushed over to our son, he was already halfway out of the door.

That was it! He just projected his anger toward our son and got physical with him. This man had been a danger to us for a long time. I'd be keeping my son in danger if I were to stay with him.

I knew from that moment on, Panda and I were no longer together. Having him take his anger out on me is one thing, but an innocent two-year-old is another. I needed to protect my son. I needed to protect my life, my housing, and my dog hiding in the other room with her tail between her legs.

I furiously started to gather his clothes and his toiletries and placed them outside of our hotel door. Since we didn't have much, it only took me a couple of minutes. By the time I was done, he hadn't had the time to drive off yet. I told him to come get it. He thought I was bluffing, so he came back up and tried to get in. But within those few short minutes, I called down the desk and told the receptionist that Panda was no longer a resident, to please reset all the keys, and that I was sorry for all the inconvenience.

I padlocked the door just in case. He must have texted me a hundred times over the next couple of hours. I had to shut my phone off to preserve my sanity. That was the longest night of my life. I kept checking the clock, anticipating my mom to come home from work. What I had just done was huge, and I needed someone to tell me it was okay. That my son and I were going to be okay. I kept thinking about how everyone was right about Panda all along. Did they see something I didn't? How did it come to this? Who did I become? How broken was I? Would this hurt ever go away? How did he get like this? Who was I going to marry?

This hurt was real. It was the worst breakup I have ever experienced.

What was everyone going to say? What was everyone going to think? I still cared what everyone else thought. Maybe that's why I stayed in this life-sucking relationship for so long. I saw the odds stacked against me, and I took it on with my head high, confident I could handle it. I failed. I failed myself, my family, and most importantly, my son. My guilt grew and grew. My heart was breaking, but I needed my brain to remain strong. Every time I felt weak, that sentence would play again in my head, and as I rocked my son to sleep with tears falling down my face and onto his back, I would say out loud over and over, "I was not given a second chance at life to live it like this."

My aunts and uncles found out about the breakup and called me. They didn't come over to see if I was okay but still expressed their opinion nevertheless. They would say things like, "Didn't you see how much your mother struggled trying to raise you on her own." Or "Marriage isn't easy. You both have to work hard together to make it work."

They thought I gave up too soon. They didn't know what was going on behind closed doors. I didn't want them to hate him like many of my former friends did. I thought I saved him from that, but instead, I looked like the bad guy. But that was okay. I could live with that because I could actually live again.

I had to hear about it from family on the holidays and when we spoke on the phone. But I was safe, and my son was safe, and my household became peaceful again.

At the hotel, I would sometimes hear others fighting through the walls and would cringe and have a quick flashback of something that resembled PTSD. I would catch myself running to the opposite side of the hotel room, locking my son in my mother's room with the door shut, and turning up the TV as loud as we needed.

Everything I was afraid of happening did happen. He slandered my name and told everyone I kicked him out to go live in his car during snowstorms, where he almost froze to death. His own father publicly attacked me at three in the morning during a drunken binge on Facebook. I had to delete 1,500 people from my Facebook friends list and only kept 500. I didn't want everyone to see me fail. I kept only those who were most important and family. He has never apologized or spoken to me since. Now I know where Panda gets it from.

For the record, I offered Panda money to stay under the same roof as us in the hotel but in a different room. I told him I never wanted him to come back into our hotel room again. I set boundaries. But how could I have kicked him out when there were vacant rooms in our hotel? Days later, we had a winter storm, and he chose not to take me up on my offer. He decided to sleep in his car in the parking lot. I think he was testing my bluff. And if I didn't cave, at least he could tell people I did this to him.

If I brought Maddox to see him at work, all his co-workers would look at me angrily. The ones who would once talk to me ran in different directions avoiding eye contact. I was shunned by all who knew us as a couple. Just when I didn't think I could feel any more alone.

Chapter 37 - Stop Looking in Rearview Mirrors

When I was with Panda, I had to drive everywhere because he only had his 350Z, a two-seater sports car that could not legally transport our two-year-old son. Whenever he wanted to see Maddox, I would have to drop him off and pick him up. My son hated going with him, but as the months turned into years, he accepted it. Now and then, he still puts up a fight but caves after knowing he won't get his way. It tore my heart open at first because I didn't know if Panda was being mean or taking his anger out on him.

Every time I left Maddox with Panda was incredibly difficult. I would drive away sobbing, knowing my son was reaching for me crying, hysterically in the arms of his father. I hoped it would get easier with time, and eventually, it did.

My mother, son, dog, and I spent a year in that hotel. It was almost like doing time in a minimum-security jail until I took up geocaching. At first, I started geocaching to escape an angry man waiting to pounce on me at home over absolutely nothing. I took my time away to escape into the woods and "recharge my batteries."

I would map out where I was going to go and check out the terrain and the sizes of the containers so I could get my son excited about new toys I didn't have to buy, and I could exchange some of the toys he no longer played with. It helped make him eager to spend time outdoors. It gave me time to digest and get rid of the mean things Panda had said to me, and it kept me fit. It was a win-win. Living in Chicopee meant new areas to explore.

Once Panda was completely out of the picture, I ran to the woods less frequently. I was able to start thinking clearly in normal environments. When he left, I instantly felt better.

You either die single, or you live long enough to see yourself as a cliché. About a month after we broke up, a "friend" started to message Panda on Facebook, flirting with him. She was making her way through my friends and exes like the stomach flu. We were the only two girls in our group who had blonde hair, so if you had a type, you would find it between the two of us. Sadly, I kept her in my life even after he told me. I was desperately lonely and had a hard time letting go of anyone who resembled something of a friend. But that didn't last long.

I was too depressed to do anything, and I didn't have any activities or friends outside the home. Meanwhile, I was still out of work while the government and I were waiting for my cancer to come back.

They put me on SSI (social security benefits) for five years, anticipating the re-arrival of the aggressive cancer. I was patiently waiting to become a patient again. This time with a two-year-old clutched around my ankle.

I couldn't help to wonder if Panda knew me while I was a "sick girl," would he have treated me so badly? At first, I thought it was a blessing he didn't know me then. I thought it spared him from seeing me at my worst. But now, I was at my worst. I went from everyone caring about me and wanting to be around me to never wanting to talk to me again. It was heartbreaking, and I often had the fleeting thought that maybe I should have let go when I had people surrounding my hospital bed. But then I would look down at my little boy and know I would rather have him by my side rather than a bunch of fake people.

It was always extra hard for me to lose anyone in my life because I grew up as an only child. I always looked at my cousins like siblings and at friends with optimistic, open arms. That feeling may have stemmed deeper. Maybe it was an absence I felt since birth when my twin passed away. Maybe that was the missing feeling I always felt tugging on my heart.

Other than having no friends, it didn't take me long to appreciate being alone after my breakup with Panda. I felt at peace about it.

I became so content that I refused to date for seven years after we split up. I wouldn't give anyone a time or day. I focused on just raising my son to be the best little man he could be. I gave him all my time and attention morning, noon, and night and he loved it.

My family didn't understand. At every family gathering, I would get questioned about whether I had met someone yet. They even asked about my sexual orientation. Finally, after the fifth year, they stopped asking. If I had only five years left on Earth, I was going to give it to my son and no one else. He needed those memories the most!

There is something beautiful about the bond between a mother and a son. I lived for that little boy just as much as he lived for me. My mother and I wasted no time in taking him on as many adventures as I could. I wanted to see the world with him and give him as many experiences as I could while I was still here. I took as many pictures as I could everywhere we went.

Every night I prayed I would see another day with him. My world rose and set in his eyes.

Chapter 38 - New Beginnings

While we were at the hotel, I received a letter from SSI telling me that my term waiting for the cancer to come back was now up. "Time to try to put the past behind you and focus on the future," my mother said. But now I had a two-year-old little boy. I had such a huge gap in my career that having to explain my absence to a potential employer may have caused me to look like a liability. And I would be denied employment. I feared I no longer looked like a good hire on paper.

I also had another problem, babysitters. Even as a child, I never liked babysitters. So I knew that option was not on the table for my son.

Panda's father was in his seventies and lived an hour and a half away. My mother was still supervising at the post office. Panda was still working full-time. My father was still out of the picture.

I knew I had to think outside of the box. I was expecting to get a check from the insurance company for my belongings from the fire. They depreciated everything owned by 75%. I was devastated. Everything I owned was in that basement since we had just moved in less than four months ago. The only irreplaceable thing was a picture of Georgie that I made sure I came back for! I found it on the very top of a pile of soot and some unrecognizable items. It was like he placed it there just for me to find it. At least I had money from the sale of my house.

Next, I started to brainstorm the jobs held in the past where I might be able to take my son with me. One was a personal care assistant job where I took care of my former stepdad. I attempted to take care of him again, but that was short-lived.

Next on the list was a tanning salon. It was one of the four jobs I had right before I got diagnosed. I knew I couldn't bring my son to work at someone else's tanning salon, so I checked to see if there were any tanning salons within a twenty-mile radius for sale. I found one in Monson that was being sold for close to nothing. And there was one in Springfield where I grew up. Monson was closer to me but further for everyone I knew.

The next day, I checked out the one in Springfield. I asked my mother to watch Maddox so I could meet with the real estate agent hired by the salon. He showed me the numbers, and I was impressed. I made an offer right there on the spot. He made a quick phone call, and it was accepted. Hallelujah, my next chapter began.

At first, I brought my son with me every day. At age two-and-a-half, he was a little distracting, and I felt bad that he no longer had play dates with me and was just stuck in a work environment. So I called around and found a wonderful lady named Anne who took him two days a week at first. Then it was three. By September, I enrolled him into preschool early with an IEP (individualized education program) that he needed due to his chronic ear infections and delayed speech.

He went to pre-K three times a week until he went to kindergarten.

This was about the same time my father passed away. He had major head trauma with an accident at work and nearly didn't make it. The doctors said he was a miracle. They had to remove half of his skull to relieve the pressure from his brain. He wasn't supposed to walk or talk after that, but he did. He pushed himself through it.

Even though he left me on my death bed, I refused to do that to him. I took time off work, and I visited him while he was in critical care and through his recovery process. He never apologized for the awful things he said and for abandoning me when I needed him the most. But I forgave him.

Before his accident, he was living with Hepatitis B and didn't realize it. By the time they caught it in the hospital, he was already stage-four, and it was progressively getting worse until it took his life several months later.

Next, I lost my grandfather, who I loved dearly and liked looking after whenever I could. We lost him the day after Christmas. I brought him to my aunt's house and cut his hair that night. It killed me to know that was the last haircut I would ever give him. I never wanted to leave him at the funeral home. My heart ripped back open when he died.

Seven months later, my uncle Tom, who was staying with us, had a severe stroke. I found him at seven in the morning on the floor. Another image I wish I could erase from my brain. My uncle was the biggest protector for my mom and me throughout our lives. He was full of fun stories from his years in the military and had a sense of understanding with God. He was truly a great man.

In the span of a year, I lost three important male figures in my life. I do not take death well, but I cannot allow my son to see me shattered, so I held my composure until I had my free time. Then I would break down in shambles, whether it was in the shower, outside, or in the basement.

I was more fortunate than ever to have both my stepdads still in my life. I needed them more now than ever. Even though my mother broke it off with my stepdad Bob, he was still very much around. He adores my son, and my son loves him just as much. We are lucky to have him in our lives.

Bob and Ray helped fill a void I didn't know I had. They are both religious men who inspire me to push myself and become successful. I think they were so hard on me as a child so they could steer me in the right direction. As much as I hated their authority as a child, I wouldn't be who I am today without them. And there is no greater feeling than knowing they are proud of me and my accomplishments.

Ten years after my cancer treatments, I took on a new title, Cancer Free. Not the sick girl. Not the girl with cancer. Ten years ago, I punched cancer in the face. As much as I would love to say that I punched cancer in the face and never looked back, I can't. I had to hit that ten-year mark to accept this. I am now ready to move on.

Speaking of moving on, my sisters all returned to my life. A year after my father passed away, my middle sister Mariah moved in with me for a year. She is now established, living in Massachusetts. She has turned more into a best friend. My youngest sister Madison graduated high school and is still out in Pennsylvania. I just sold her my old Jeep. She is turning twenty-one this year. I cannot wait to get closer to her. And lastly, my sister, who is eight years younger than me, has followed in my father's footsteps. He treated her like a child to party with, so unfortunately she is doing time in prison. Life is what you make of it, right?

I just applied to go back to AIC and get my Master of Arts in counseling psychology, and I couldn't be prouder of myself and my accomplishments. I was even on a date last night, which is also a big step for me. I am accepting the fact that I am promised a future, so I might as well start planning for it.

I will never forget what cancer has taught me. Before I had cancer, I wasn't really living. I was just going through the motions. I would never look at a cloud or a flower like I do today. I am aware of my surroundings, and I live in the moment fully, with admiration and appreciation. It is like my senses awoke. Almost dying taught me how to live.

"So write down your story. Write it down over and over again. And once you realize it's only that, a story. Once you realize it's all in the past and you can't change any of it and they're now only words on a sheet of paper that you can throw away in the trash can. That's when we can try to figure out who you are and who you'll be." -Chuck Palahniuk (Invisible Monsters)